An Innovative Economic Incentive Model for Improvement of the Working Environment in Europe

EF/95/18/EN

An Innovative Economic Incentive Model for Improvement of the Working Environment in Europe

Stephen Bailey
Kirsten Jørgensen
Christian Koch
Wolfgang Krüger
Henrik Litske

**European Foundation
for the Improvement of Living and Working Conditions**
Loughlinstown House
Shankill, Co. Dublin, Ireland
Tel: + 353 1 282 6888
Fax: + 353 1 282 6456

Cataloguing data can be found at the end of this publication

Luxembourg: Office for Official Publications of the European Communities, 1995

ISBN 92-827-4912-6

Printed in Ireland

Summary

This report describes a European model for economic motivation targeting the improvement of health and safety at work. Several different types of economic incentives are contained within the one model.

The proposed system operates within a framework of compulsory industrial injury insurance paid by the employer. However, the incentives aim to mobilize a number of social parties inside and outside the individual enterprise.

Based on considerations of the dynamics of European economies, the primary tools suggested are premium graduation with a bonus system, investment aid and a marketing label to denote excellence in the working environment.

Premium graduation could be based on the calculation of both existing and future risks and thus be proactive in nature. The basic idea would be to assign each enterprise a gross premium and then offer possibilities of a premium reduction or bonus. The premium could be composed of three elements to reflect base, sector and work function aspects of the working environment.

The highest level - the gross premium - would be assigned to enterprises operating close to the minimum requirements of health and safety legislation. Bonuses are then awarded to enterprises operating to higher standards.

The bonus system could comprise three sub-bonuses: general, specified and individual sub-bonuses. A general sub-bonus would be given to enterprises when they have improved health and safety, and would be awarded by the responsible organisation without a special application by the enterprise. Specified bonuses would be centrally designed to address recognised health and safety problems in a sector and would be awarded upon application. Individual bonuses would be given upon application, to enterprises with individual problems who co-operate to develop novel solutions.

Investment aid incentives could be made available to enterprises interested in investments that improve health and safety and showing willingness to develop these improvements. The development could be described in a contract and supported by health and safety professionals.

Award of the marketing label for excellence in the working environment could be related to the bonus system and be offered to enterprises that obtain a specified amount of bonus.

A major consideration behind this proposal is the diversity of enterprises. It is necessary to consider differences between sectors and sizes of enterprises, differences in technology and in the corporate culture of the organisations. In part, the sub-bonus system addresses these different needs. Additionally, a special programme is proposed for small enterprises.

Documentation and evaluation routines necessary for the operation of the incentive model are detailed. Information about causes of known and future risks must be collated from several sources. Information about the consequences of accidents or exposures, the workforce, the enterprises and the actual work are all necessary components.

Options for the organisation of the body responsible for the incentive model are described. Key criteria are the effectiveness of administration, including how visits are prioritized and the procedures for complaints and appeals.

Throughout the report, the necessary flexibility across national systems is emphasised. The incentives could be implemented in a number of different ways and embedded in different organisations.

In the final chapter, practical issues concerning the implementation of the proposals are discussed.

Preface

The social partners, governmental authorities, politicians, researchers and insurance companies all over Europe are increasingly looking for new ways to improve the working environment beyond the minimum level required by law. One important mechanism for doing so is by the economic motivation of companies. Several existing insurance schemes for compensation of injured employees have built-in economic incentives through employers' contributions which are based on the risks in the workplace. Other countries do not have such systems in place but are analysing the options.

To assist the policy makers in this process at national and European level the Foundation established in 1993 a European Forum where member states can exchange views and experiences on the topic. Based on these discussions a multidisciplinary working party has prepared four publications for the Foundation. The first report was an extensive catalogue of the major economic incentive systems in operation internationally (see Reference 1). Advantages and disadvantages of these different systems were analyzed and discussed and the conclusions were summarized in a booklet (Reference 2). Knowledge and experience was extended further through a seminar with Eastern Europe in October 1994 held in Warsaw. Interesting new models are being developed here (Reference 3).

This report is the fourth publication. Based on the experiences of the earlier phases of the project the working party assisted by a Steering Group has developed elements of an innovative economic incentive model. This theoretical model would need further development and testing. It would also need to be adapted to national tradition and structures before it could be implemented. The purpose of this proposal is only to serve as a source of inspiration to those policy makers who seek to improve or change existing economic incentive schemes or who are considering introducing new systems of this kind.

It is our hope that this report will contribute to the improvement of the future working environment in Europe.

Clive Purkiss
Director

Eric Verborgh
Deputy Director

Acknowledgements

This report has been prepared for the European Foundation for the Improvement of Living and Working Conditions by a team comprising Ms K Jørgensen, Mr C Koch, Prof Dr W Krüger, Mr H Litske and Mr S R Bailey.

Kirsten Jørgensen MSc (Eng) PhD is head of the Department of Analysis and Documentation at the Danish National Working Environment Service in Copenhagen.

Christian Koch MSc (Eng) is Assistant Professor at the Institute for Technology and Society, Unit for Technology Assessment, Technical University of Denmark. He is attached to the Unit for the Working Environment and the Centre for Interdisciplinary Studies of Technology Management.

Prof Dr Wolfgang Krüger has degrees in engineering and economics and is Dean of the Faculty of Safety Engineering at the University of Wuppertal, Germany.

Henrik Litske MA (Economics) is Research Manager for the European Foundation for the Improvement of Living and Working Conditions, Shankill, Co.Dublin, Ireland and is responsible for the Foundation's project on economic incentives.

Steve Bailey MSc (Pollution) Dip Occ Hyg CChem FRSC FIOH MIOSH is Past President of the Institute of Occupational Hygienists and now runs his own consultancy *Flexpro,* in the United Kingdom.

K Jørgensen and C Koch originated the text for Chapters 1, 3, 4, 5 and 6 whilst Prof. Dr. Krüger originated Chapter 2 on the application of economic incentives. S Bailey edited the manuscript.

The working party would like to thank all those who contributed information and comments during the course of the project, in particular the members of the steering group listed below.

STEERING GROUP

Mr J P A Bakkum	Ministerie van Sociale Zaken en Werkegelegenheid, Netherlands
Mr R Waeyaert	NCMV, De Organisatie voor Zelfstandige Ondernemers, Belgium
Mr M Sapir	European Trade Union Bureau for Health and Safety, Belgium
Mr J R Biosca de Sagastuy	European Commission, Luxembourg
Mr M Heselmans	Ministerie van Tewerkstelling en Arbeid, Belgium
Mr D Le Page	EUROGIP, France
Prof D Koradecka	Central Institute of Labour Protection, Poland

Contents

Introduction 1

1.1 Background

The purpose of this report is to describe a model consisting of a number of economic incentive methods which may have positive effects on the working environment.

Economic incentive methods are methods which financially reward those enterprises that ensure and develop good and safe working conditions.

The report takes as its starting point the conclusions from the earlier phases of the project, which the European Foundation for the Improvement of Living and Working Conditions began in 1993. In Phase 1, existing economic incentive systems throughout Europe and Canada were researched and catalogued.[Ref 1] They were then analysed and compared during Phase 2, which is documented in the booklet "Economic Incentives to Improve the Working Environment" [Ref 2] published by the Foundation. A principal conclusion of the study was that the systems currently applied can be improved. This launched a debate as to which incentive methods might have better effects than those used at present.

The debate has been led by the Foundation's project Steering Group, whose membership is drawn from all over Europe and reflects a variety of experiences and viewpoints.

To further the debate, an international colloquium on economic incentive schemes was held in Warsaw in October 1994, organised jointly by the Foundation and the Polish Central Institute for Labour Protection.[Ref 3] Here, East and West European nations exchanged ideas and experiences. New systems being developed in Eastern Europe were described, and speakers from the project team presented their preliminary ideas.

The outcome of these deliberations forms the basis for this report. The report was prepared by a small team of authors working under the guidance of the Steering Group. Although the authors held differing perspectives on how incentives should be applied, they were nevertheless able to reach a consensus on the material presented.

Those economic motivation methods that are advocated are a combination of newly developed methods with existing practical experience. The report describes how such methods can motivate enterprises, how the working environment and the efforts made may be evaluated, and the organisation that is required at the national level for the methods to work in everyday life. Finally, the implementation of the methods is discussed.

The report concentrates on how to bring about economic motivation as an element of industrial injury insurance. However, the report is not intended to be exhaustive as regards economic measures, forms of organisation or methods of evaluation. Nor is it prescriptive. Rather it is a toolbox, a collection of ideas which have already found favour with a wide body of opinion, and are now presented for further debate.

The report should thus be seen as a source of inspiration for re-evaluating existing systems and for developing new ones. Development efforts in several fields will be required before the methods can be applied in practice.

1.2 Conclusions from Phases 1 and 2

The main conclusions from the study of existing economic incentive methods were as follows:

1. That safety and health is a public good and desire which cannot be obtained through normal market economy mechanisms.

2. A well-designed system will motivate employers to improve the working environment if it offers them an economic advantage.

3. Most systems today are based on historical measures, viz. reported injuries which have led to the payment of compensation. Such systems have proved to have only a limited impact on preventive work.

4. Critical elements in the design of a new system are:
   - the size of the incentive, i.e. the economic advantage/cost.
   - the efficiency of the system as regards measuring and demonstrating improvements to health and safety and responsiveness to the individual enterprise.
   - how well the system covers both *health* and *safety* (i.e. the risk of both diseases and accidents).
   - the extent and amount of compensation in connection with occupational injuries.
   - the degree of protection provided to small and medium-sized enterprises (SME's) against statistical fluctuations in incentive payments.
   - the administrative functioning of the system and the costs involved.
   - whether it takes into account the special issues of SME's.

5. There is a need for the design of a statistical recording system covering safety and health problems and particularly the incidence of occupational injuries.

6. Existing systems operate with only a limited definition of industrial accidents and diseases. New schemes could operate with a more generalized definition of occupational injuries, including

occupational accidents, occupational diseases, other acute injuries, attrition and other nuisances resulting in frequent absence due to illness.

> **Occupational Injuries**
> We use the term "occupational injuries" throughout this report in the broad sense to include disease and illness as well as accidents. We will discuss the concept more fully in Section 4.1.

1.3 Basic preconditions

Based on these main conclusions, this report takes the following preconditions as its starting point. The preconditions are emphasised in order to make clear the restrictions assumed. They can, however, be overruled in/by specific national contexts:

1. The employer is the legal entity who will benefit from the economic motivation. Hence the employer is the central target for the incentives. The proposed methods are, however, intended to make use of the enterprise's social resources. They set the stage for co-operation between the parties at the enterprise on preventive activities.

> **Enterprise**
> Throughout the report we use the term "enterprise" to denote all kinds of organisations targetted by the incentive scheme, regardless of legal or financial status and whether they are in the private or public sector.

2. The economic motivation is aimed at improving the working environment beyond what is required by working environment legislation.

As improvements beyond the minimum legal requirements are expensive, there is a clear need for economic motivation to promote achievement of these higher standards. It is therefore proposed that economic motivation should be a supplement to the working environment legislation rather than a replacement.

However, economic motivation could, if desired, be targetted on enterprises that operate below the standard required by working environment legislation.

3. **The body responsible for economic incentive methods will essentially be a public, semipublic, independent or controlled private organisation.**

We will concentrate on a situation where employers pay and receive benefits from a central authority or institution depending on their actions in relation to the goals and requirements that have been set. It has turned out that a free insurance market is not capable of providing an adequate basis for prevention since the individual insurance company only insures itself in relation to its own risk which therefore means non-uniform conditions for enterprises.

However, it should be stressed at this point that the report does not recommend only one possible organisational form: on the contrary, it suggests several alternatives described in Section 5 of the report.

4. **The economic motivation shall only be intended to *prevent* occupational injuries rather than trying to remedy what has happened. The motivational effect therefore has to point forward.**

When it comes to inducing motivation to improve safety and health at work, i.e. motivation to eliminate the risks which may lead to injuries or diseases, the starting point and the basis for the motivational methods must be the actual safety conditions in the enterprises. These dictate the risks of future accidents and development of diseases. The sources of risk have to be reduced. This goal reaches beyond those of the existing insurance systems whose primary emphasis is on securing compensation payments for injuries that have already happened. The existing insurance systems can therefore base themselves on measurements of the outcome of past working conditions, whereas the proposed system cannot.

5. **The motivation "pointing forward" means that the system must promote efforts instead of results.**

This follows from the fact that it is a reduction of *risk* which is in focus, not a reduction of recorded absence due to illness or number of accidents. The latter should be included in the system, but is not the earliest possible "signal" on which to base prevention. In addition, the number of recorded accidents in small and medium-sized enterprises is too small to provide a reliable basis for prevention activities.

6. **The motivational methods ought to be of a positive nature. Systems should ensure that those who do something to improve safety and health are rewarded, instead of punishing those who do nothing.**

The model is premised on the idea that positive co-operation is the best way forward. It is assumed throughout that the economic incentive is related to enterprises that want to co-operate with the responsible organisation. Therefore we only briefly describe premium augmentation as a punishment for poor working environments and sanctions towards enterprises acting illegally in relation to the legislation on the workers' compensation system (see Section 5, Organisation).

7. **The economic advantage to the enterprises and the improvement of health and safety at work must have a visible correlation, so as to leave no doubt about when the advantage is there and why.**

Visibility and transparency promotes direct motivation but also contributes to strengthening competition concerning the working environment among enterprises in a specific sector.

8. **Moreover, it must be quite clear which initiatives in relation to the working environment will result in an economic advantage for the individual enterprise. The advantage must be given immediately after concrete safety and health improvements have been achieved.**

Points 7, 8 and 9 will all have an effect on how the economic incentives will work in practice in relation to the social partners of the enterprise.

9. **There must be no direct relationship between the reporting or compensation of injuries and the economic incentive to the employer.**

Such a relationship would only motivate the employer negatively not to report injuries and thus put the victim in a poorer position.

Information on injuries that have occurred is vital to the statistical calculations and documentation of the risk factors giving rise to the injuries, but information on injuries can only be used indirectly in connection with the assessment of the risk at the individual enterprise.

1.4 Target Groups

Extensive understanding by the responsible body of target groups among the enterprises is of vital importance to the interaction between the enterprises and the responsible body. This primarily means an understanding of the dissimilarities between enterprises and also a grasp of the enterprise as a social system. The concept of the enterprise as a **social system** implies understanding the enterprise as an organism in which different parties interact: the employer, the management, the employees, shop stewards, the internal safety organisation, the safety representatives. This interaction is of critical importance to the effectiveness of external motivation, and the methods of motivation must be adapted to it. We will refer to the social system in an individual enterprise as its "**corporate culture**".

Decision making in enterprises is influenced by the corporate culture. Decisions are taken not only as a result of interpretation of the market, competitors and other economic factors but also as a result of beliefs, values and legal requirements. This includes the organisation's attitude towards working environment problems and activities.

Economic incentives aim at moving the borderline for what are considered attractive activities by the corporate culture.

Many working environment improvements might in fact turn out to be profitable by themselves when one includes factors like absence due to illness and employee motivation. The profitability of improvements is, however, not the only criterion for enterprise. Incentives are thus a means of communicating with the social system of the company and influencing its values and attitude towards health and safety problems. Table 1 below summarizes these considerations in terms of whether the enterprise is willing to work actively or not.

Motivating the employer is not sufficient although the economic motivation is formally aimed at him. On the contrary, the incentive methods must be aimed at the entire corporate culture if they are to ensure optimum motivation. The workers' council and the health and safety representatives and/or other collective representatives of the employees could be considered the second most important social partners to relate to when establishing preventive action.

Furthermore the individual employees could be motivated through direct or indirect involvement in the preventive activities. On the other hand, direct economic motivation of employees should not be offered. This is because the employer has the principal responsibility for the organisation of the work and its execution. Therefore, the employer has the best opportunity to explore ways of providing incentives to the employees. In addition, the proposed system is in the nature of a social security scheme.

Another central determining feature of the corporate culture is the size of enterprise. It has been shown in several investigations that **small enterprises** present a specific problem in terms of accident rates (higher than average), the lack of health and safety organisation and the infrequent contact with external authorities. These enterprises often work without formalized internal planning and with one person as a central figure in all decision making.

When referring to small enterprises it is important to emphasize that this is here taken to mean less than around 50 employees. In some countries and sectors the limits for establishing a safety organisation are even lower. Experience shows that these enterprises have to be approached in a specific way. One example is that some small enterprises are proud of their non-bureaucratic form of organisation. An approach to these companies that implies substantial application (or other) paperwork might only create resistance.

Although it is attractive to have a simple system with few formal procedures, this will in practice be at odds with the many different preventive tasks for which motivation is required within the enterprises.

This report is based on the following understanding of target groups:

O Some enterprises are typical of their sector as regards production processes, technology and materials used, manpower and the resulting working environment problems.

O Others are far from this average because they use other technologies, or because their working environment is exceptionally good or poor.

O Some enterprises have an active corporate culture that promotes health and safety, others have a passive one and others again have an antagonistic corporate culture as far as external motivation and the prevention of occupational injuries are concerned.

O Finally, some small enterprises might not be able to respond, or be interested in responding, to external motivation unless it is shaped specifically for their form of work and corporate culture.

Table 1 summarises the main situations which economic incentive methods must target.

Target group	
Type of enterprise	Corporate culture
Enterprises with standard problems	Willing to work actively or passive
Enterprises with standard problems looking for solutions	Willing to work actively
Enterprises with individual problems knowing the solution	Willing to work actively
Enterprises with individual problems not knowing the solution	Willing to work actively
Small enterprises	All types

Table 1: Target groups for incentives

Similarly, the responsible body will in its evaluation and control activities distinguish between enterprises with a high, medium and low risk level compared with the sector. It will arrange its activities accordingly, including the frequency of visits, special evaluations and special incentives.

The health and safety problems in the target enterprises which are to be tackled by the incentives include the whole spectrum of health and safety issues, such as:

○ Physical environment (i.e. light, noise)

○ Psychological

○ Ergonomic

○ Chemical

○ Biological

○ Acute hazards (e.g. mechanical and electrical)

and the solutions to be promoted include measures which are:

○ Technical

○ Organisational

○ Educational.

This broad understanding of problems and solutions is necessary if the incentive is to help the target enterprises achieve real improvements in prevention across sectors of industry and commerce with very different working environments.

Furthermore it is necessary to understand the working environment as a continually changing issue. New machines, tools, products, raw materials, chemicals, recruits etc. all contribute to change in the workplace. The introduction of these is not only a result of market forces. Other dynamics are also active such as public debate, governmental regulation, fashion-phenomena and others.

Some of these changes go on month by month, others intermittently, but this dynamism underlines the necessity to re-evaluate the schemes continually in order to meet the reality of the target enterprises.

Principles of Economic Incentives

2

2.1 Introduction

Some basic reflections are necessary on the effects and side effects of possible incentives, before a special incentive method can be designed and recommended.

Risk reduction in the enterprise can be realised by a health and safety programme which includes

○ technical measures

○ organisational measures

○ instruction and training of employees and employers.

These types of instruments can be used in various combinations to promote safety and health. Technical measures normally can be applied to investment decisions of the enterprise that are taken for predominantly economic reasons. Therefore we start with the technical aspect, and we shall deal with organisation and training separately.

The questions of training and instruction are regulated in detail in many European countries by legal requirements. Directive 89/391/EEC (the "framework directive"), when in force, will guarantee uniform minimum standards. An important additional measure in this field could then be the introduction of "safety and health circles". The promotion of this instrument will be discussed later in Section 3.7.

Gains (or cost reductions) for an enterprise can be obtained by various means, e.g.

1. tax reductions
2. subsidies of various kinds
3. influencing the availability of capital
4. reduction of insurance premiums
5. marketing assistance.

Of course each of these instruments can be used in the negative direction, too, e.g. increasing taxes and premiums, putting extra loads on "bad" products, etc., but we feel that the state should not explicitly "punish" the lack of activities in excess of the legal requirements. Such a procedure might also raise constitutional problems, at least in some of the member states.

2.2 The instruments

2.2.1 Taxes and Subsidies

Technical measures for the improvement of the working environment are, as a rule, connected with investment decisions by the enterprise. Economic theory has examined in great detail different instruments for stimulating investment, from subsidies on interest rates to direct payments. Our point here is not to *stimulate* investment, but to exercise *an influence on the mode* of the investment: if the enterprise has decided to buy a machine it should be encouraged to buy the less hazardous or less stressful machine. For this purpose some countries have developed programmes like the German "Humanisierung der Arbeit" (humanisation of work), where innovative models for better working conditions are sponsored by the government. This type of incentive is well established and widely practised, so we do not need to treat it here. We are interested in an incentive model not for the development of innovations but to modify routine investment decisions.

Taxes, which are mainly meant to achieve revenues for the state, can also be modified to influence private economic behaviour. If taxes are used for that purpose, it is widely accepted that they should not interfere with the freedom of private economic decisions and that they must not affect competition. These conditions make them less fit for our purpose: if a tax reduction is offered to employers who invest in equipment that is less hazardous than legally required, this does not affect the competition among the users of the equipment, because every company can have the same tax privilege. However it would noticeably affect the competition among the producers of the equipment. This can be illustrated by considering the market for machines of equal capabilities but with different noise levels (see Box).

Effect of Taxation on Competition

If a noisy and a less noisy machine can be produced at equal cost (and, while competition is effective, be sold at the same price), there is no need for intervention by the state. The market itself would bring about the desired effect because if one can buy a machine or a machine plus extra positive effects at the same price, no rationally acting individual would buy the machine without the "extras".

If the noisy machine (which, *nota bene*, meets the legal requirements) is produced (and sold) more cheaply than the less noisy one, a tax reduction would have to compensate for the price difference (and possible differences in running costs) to encourage the rationally acting employer to purchase the less noisy machine. But then the market is heavily affected: the producer of the "noisy" machine would at least lose a substantial part of his share of the market. If the competitor with the less noisy machines is big enough or can grow fast enough, the noisy machines might even be totally excluded from the market though they are strictly within the legal requirements. Such an intervention by the state is obviously not compatible with the economic system of the EU member states.

Moreover, in the EU there are still many different systems of taxation. Even if harmonisation is proceeding, it might be difficult to modify these different tax systems so that they all have an equal effect on the markets. So even if the distortion of competition in the national markets were to be accepted for the benefit of improving working conditions, the resulting different tax loads in the member states would probably constitute an obstacle for free trade within the common market.

This applies to direct tax variations as well as to any other method of influencing the tax load (such as special rates of depreciation, permission to accumulate tax-reduced operational reserves, etc.). This applies further to any type of subsidy that influences the price ratio between "good" and "bad" equipment (from payments in cash to subsidies on interest rates). We therefore do not need to discuss these methods further.

We also do not have to discuss the specific problems, in connection with the technique of tax imposition, that necessarily would be connected with most methods of subsidising "good" equipment. It is sufficient to point out that the fiscal authorities normally cannot easily react to technical differences, which they cannot judge by their own expertise. Variations of tax load in favour of improvement of the working environment would therefore require either an additional administration or co-operation between fiscal authorities and e.g. labour inspectorates, which might not be easy to establish in all member states.

2.2.2 Availability of capital

Especially for small and medium sized enterprises the availability of capital can be a problem. Unlike large companies, smaller ones often suffer from lack of assets to cover additional credit. Therefore a system could be developed that makes credit available with little or no security ("risk capital") to companies who seek to meet certain safety and health standards. This can, but does not have to, be combined with direct subsidies on the interest rates. Of course placing a credit at someone's disposal with little security can be a method of subsidising the interest rate, too, though an indirect one. Sometimes, however, a company cannot get credit for investment at any reasonable rate. Then the mere availability of "risk capital" at market rates can be incentive enough.

Such a system would not directly affect the competition among the users of equipment, because again every company has the same chance to get under-secured credit. But there are, of course, indirect effects: on the one hand it might slightly support small and medium sized enterprise, because the larger companies as a rule have easier access to the capital market. On the other hand it could be a (slight) handicap for those who participate, because they have to purchase the "good" equipment, that very often has higher running costs, e.g. additional filters, more expensive lubricants. Therefore their costs would be somewhat higher than that of a competitive company with enough security that buys the cheaper-to-operate "bad" equipment. This difference in cost could be compensated by slightly reducing the interest rate.

If the credit is given at market rates (or just below, to compensate for the higher operating costs), the influence on the market of the equipment can also be kept small: the price difference between the "good" and "bad" products is not compensated. Only additional demand, that could not be realised without the intervention, would meet the "good" products. Actual or desired safety and health standards could be certified by the industrial inspection services, which already exist in most member states or have to be installed according to Framework Directive 89/391/EEC; therefore no new bureaucracy has to be set up.

If this instrument is to be combined with a subsidy, the possible spectrum reaches from subsidies on interest rates, as mentioned above, to the conversion of the loan into a grant, if the improvement of working conditions reaches a certain predetermined level. This means that the "tuning" of the instrument could be very fine.

There are some more advantages to this method:

○ It could be installed in every member state individually but could be handled on the EU level, too.

○ In the case of an EU-solution it could help to harmonise safety and health standards, since the conditions for credit could be fixed by the EU.

○ It could be combined with subsidies of various kinds and thus could offer an additional instrument for economic policy.

○ It could not only be "tuned" very precisely in small steps, but could also be combined with "ceilings" for number of employees, capital or other structural characteristics.

○ It fits perfectly into the EU's set of instruments, so that the know-how and the administration are easily available.

○ It therefore might be put through easily.

2.2.3 Premium variations

Premium variations are widely applied at present, but do not seem to have much incentive effect so long as they are coupled with the *outcomes* of safety and health activities (as discussed in detail in the booklet "Economic Incentives to Improve the Working Environment" [Ref 2]). Traditionally, premiums are set to recover costs already incurred in the compensation of past events ("the pay-as-you-go" system). Therefore, a large portion of premium revenues has to be collected independently of the current accident occurrence or risk situation. The insurance institutions, private or public, normally do not have wide enough margins to provide a sufficient incentive.

For the discussion of the effects of premium variation we have to distinguish between compulsory and voluntary insurance and, in the case of compulsory insurance, between monopolistic or non-monopolistic market structures.

a) voluntary insurance

If the accident insurance is voluntary, the insurance companies may vary their premiums at will. A political influence on a multitude of insurance companies to make them co-ordinate their premium policy could be inconsistent with a market economy. Moreover, in the Single European market one member state might not be able to force insurers from other member states to participate in such a co-ordination.

If the insurance market is competitive, premium (= price) variations are the most important means of competition. No insurer would take the risk of losing significant parts of his share in the market by e.g. raising prices for political reasons. Some insured companies, especially the big ones, could be even driven out of the insurance system, covering the damages without help, as do the public institutions in some countries (e.g. in Germany): it has to be kept in mind that insurance does not, as a rule, change the expected value of damages but only its distribution over time. If the financial assets of an institution are big enough to compensate for peak loads, no insurance is needed.

As long as there is no fairly uniform compulsory accident insurance system in all member states of the EU, premium variations for promoting the improvement of working conditions cannot be recommended. They would not only be difficult to enforce, but could disturb competition among companies in countries with compulsory and voluntary insurance.

b) compulsory insurance

If a uniform system of compulsory accident insurance can be installed in the EU, then it depends on the details of the system as to whether and how premium variations would work. If there were a multitude of insurance bodies, as e.g. in Germany, then it would depend on the legal situation whether uniform premium variations could be enforced. At present in Germany there are 35 insurance bodies in the safety and health field, which are obliged by law to vary their premium according to the number or severity of accidents, but the methods applied differ significantly (see the system descriptions in the "Catalogue of Incentive Systems for the Improvement of the Working Environment", published by the European Foundation 1994[Ref 1]). Most of the variations remain too small to be a real incentive.

We shall now consider a system with one (and only one) insurance body in each country (or with an instrument to make a multitude of bodies act uniformly). Variations are coupled to improvements of the working conditions. Up to now, the premium variations as a rule are coupled to the outcomes, i.e. to accident rates instead. We have already pointed out that, due to statistical limitations, this can lead to considerable disadvantages for small and medium sized enterprise.

If in such a system the premium variations become large enough to be a real incentive, some constitutional problems may arise with respect to the negative side of the variations. We are talking, *nota bene*, about incentives for additional measures, not about enforcing the law. The question is whether a compulsory insurance scheme should be allowed to "punish" its members for behaviour which is strictly legal. This is questionable, and therefore we suggest positive incentives only, i.e. premium reduction in return for risk reduction.

This is already done with great success by fire insurance companies: they reduce their premium (independently of the actual damages) according to certain precautions taken by the insuree. If, e.g., a company in Germany has its own fire brigade, the premium can go down by as much as 40% (depending on the number and availability of staff, training and equipment of the fire brigade). Here we have a premium variation as a function of risk, not of statistical coincidence. In the field of labour safety and health one could offer a bonus for reducing risks below the legally admissible limits. If, for example, equipment with lower noise is employed, the premium could be reduced by a specified percentage, since the risk of damage claims for loss of hearing is objectively lower.

This is easy for a "one-insurer system" because all claims pass through the one insurance company regardless of the employee's job history. If a multitude of insurers exist with responsibility for different branches of the economy, e.g. in Germany, then an adjustment fund would have to be set up. For instance, there are branches of industry where the proportion of older workers is considerably above average, because employees try to find easier work when they get older. So employees perhaps damage their health in one branch while they are young but the claim is made in another branch later. In a "pay-as-you-go" system this would in any case disturb the market allocation, because it would burden one branch with the "consumption of human health" of another branch.

If the insurer varies his premium according to risk, this would, again, influence the market for equipment, but this time it is not done by the state, but by an institution which acts according to its own market conditions. This is within the laws of a market economy: markets are regularly affected by events in other markets. For the insurance company the bonus is rational, because the application of low noise equipment reduces the probability of work induced sickness and thus the expenditure on compensation. Insurance premiums ought to reflect the expected value of the damages, therefore a premium reduction for reduced risk is in accordance with the principles of both insurance and the market economy.

2.2.4 Marketing assistance

The "mildest" (but not necessarily the less effective) form of intervention into working conditions could be a system of marketing assistance for qualifying companies. Like the widespread certificates of environmental non-objection or the symbols for excellence in quality assurance, a symbol could be created for excellence in labour safety and health. This could be used as a marketing argument for the products or (especially) services of the company.

Several implementation methods could be considered including audits and certification related to health and safety legislation. Or, as proposed in the next section, it could be used for increasing the effects of other instruments by combining it with e.g. a certain level of premium/bonus.

2.2.5 Support for organisational improvements

The last point leads us to the "non-technical" mechanisms for improving safety and health in the company. As stated above, safety and health depend not only on the technical conditions in the enterprise, but also on its organisation and on the behaviour of its members.

In this field the effects are extremely difficult to determine. Normally regulations require what is thought to be an efficient safety and health organisation. But while e.g. lower noise, less pollution or less heavy loads can be measured (*ceteris paribus*) in terms of risk for the employees, no method is known to correlate choices of safety organisation directly with the insured risks. Since we are talking about "extra" efforts, it would be necessary to combine certain additional organisational provisions with certain incentives. We shall discuss this point by distinguishing between *safety and health organisation* and *safety by organisation*.

Speaking about the safety and health organisation first, we have to admit that we know next to nothing about its cost-effectiveness. If an employer meets e.g. the requirements of the Framework Directive (89/391/EEC) by appointing the necessary safety staff, one cannot predict whether additional risk reduction would be achieved by having extra safety personnel. We cannot even be sure that by having additional personnel we do not change the effectiveness of the safety organisation for the worse: part of each organisation's activities are directed inwards, and it is known that this portion varies by steps. Additional staff may, in other words, cause more need for co-ordination within an organisation than they add to the organisation's ability to solve "outside" problems. Since it is nearly impossible to guess what effect additional personnel might have, an incentive would have to be linked to other changes.

In the field of the safety organisation such a change might be the improvement of supervision, be it the length and number of inspections or the application of elaborate techniques such as modern hazard analysis. Such improvements require additional manpower and therefore are expensive. A larger company could do it by additional personnel, a smaller one would have to "buy" external expertise.

Though the improvement of safety supervision and inspections most certainly reduces risks for the employees, the "dose-effect relationship" is very difficult to determine. Therefore this is more a field for direct subsidies than for premium variations (which should, as stated above, reflect the actual risk reduction as precisely as possible).

Improvements in safety and health organisation could be combined with marketing assistance, too: since the necessary audit checks the technical and the organisational aspects of the enterprise, a certain number of "points" could be given for meeting the legal requirements and others for "extra efforts". So on the one hand it could be ensured that no company could advertise using the proposed "sign for excellence in labour safety and health", unless its safety organisation is, at least, within the limits of the regulations. On the other hand a company could be awarded the sign for even minor technical improvements if the safety organisation is improved simultaneously.

The situation regarding the prediction of effects is better with respect to safety and health *by* organisation. Here in some cases the effects of organisational improvements are better known. For instance, job rotation can be organised in such a way that it reduces parameters such as sick leave, absenteeism and also accident risks. An employer who reduces repetitive work through job rotation and specified time scheduling can improve working conditions in a measurable way. In this case, premium variations could be applied to stimulate the organisational improvements.

The ergonomic variables of stress and load on the one hand, and recovery on the other hand, seem to be the best points of reference for determination of economic incentives for the time being. The aspect of perception, which also adds considerably to safety and health, can be normally influenced more by technical than by organisational changes.

2.2.6 Promotion of safety and health education and training

Lack of knowledge about the effects of safety and health education and training makes the application of economic incentives very difficult in this field, too. Neither the time spent under instruction, nor the "knowledge" of the employees about or their attitude towards safety and health topics, are reliable indicators of their safety behaviour.

Moreover the outcomes of safety education are very difficult to measure. The only variable that could be determined comparatively easily, the time for instruction and training, is the least useful: too many conditions determine the effects of instruction, so that nothing can be said about the resulting risk reduction connected with a certain training time.

Nevertheless additional safety and health education and training should be encouraged by offering economic incentives. Very often a technical and/or organisational improvement can only be effective (or, at least, be more effective) if it is accompanied by safety training and instruction.

Here again, because of the uncertainties about the resulting risk reduction, direct subventions (which cover the additional cost) should be offered rather than premium reductions. Again we cannot recommend tax variations, because of the different systems of taxation in the EU. Therefore the best way would be direct payments. Of course, the "risk capital", mentioned above, could be offered more cheaply, too, for those who combine their investment with the introduction of additional safety education and training.

As additional safety and health education and training necessarily increases the cost of the enterprise, no distortion of competition is to be expected if someone encourages these activities by economic incentives, as long as the incentives only compensate for the cost difference.

Application of Incentives

3.1 Introduction

3.1.1 The Tools Proposed

Following the definition of problems and target groups in Section 1, it is seen to be crucial that an economic incentive model consists of several different methods or tools if it is to function effectively. Section 2 highlighted a number of possible approaches including financing, motivation and integration into marketing. It also implies that they should be used to support different aspects of preventive actions.

A central conclusion that can be drawn from Section 2 is that the economic incentives could operate within a framework of compulsory industrial injury insurance taken out by the employer. The finance for the incentives would then be obtained from premiums paid on the basis of an assessment of risks at the enterprises.

The different methods proposed are described in this section, finishing with a discussion on how incentives can be co-ordinated with other initiatives aimed at enterprises. We will not discuss in this chapter how the organisation behind the insurance system should be established or how the evaluation can be done for each of the incentive methods. These are the topics of the following two sections.

> **EMMI-body**
> Throughout the rest of the report we use the abbreviation "EMMI-body" to denote the responsible organisation behind the proposed incentive scheme. EMMI stands for "European Model for Motivation by Incentives".

The methods that will be proposed are designed to meet the specific problems of each of the target groups as discussed in the Introduction. Those we will discuss are:

○ Premium graduation
○ Bonuses for efforts
○ A special scheme for small enterprises
○ Investment aid
○ A marketing label.

The incentive methods are listed roughly in priority order. Their application to the target groups is summarised in Table 2.

Premium graduation is the most basic and general tool. Bonuses and investment aids are intended to be supplementary to premium graduation. The priority to be accorded to the special scheme for small enterprises can be proportionate to the number of small enterprises and their contribution to health and safety problems.

Labelling is a voluntary method. It would give the enterprises that have achieved specified objectives in a given year an opportunity to use a label signifying this in their marketing activities.

Furthermore two sorts of sanctions are considered in the proposals made in the report. First is the option of sanctions towards enterprises that do not meet the standards required by health and safety legislation. This is considered below. Second is the tools needed for the EMMI-body to create a proper framework for co-operation with the enterprises. This type of sanction is described in Section 5, Organisation.

Target group		Incentive Method					
Type of enterprise	Corporate culture	Premium graduation	General Bonus	Bonus for specified efforts	Bonus for individual efforts	Investment aid	Small enterprise scheme
Enterprises with standard problems	Willing to work actively or passive	x	x				
Enterprises with standard problems looking for solutions	Willing to work actively	x	x	x			
Enterprises with individual problems knowing the solution	Willing to work actively	x	x		x		
Enterprises with individual problems not knowing the solution	Willing to work actively	x	x			x	
Small enterprises	All types	x	x	x	x	x	x

Table 2: Proposed incentives for different target groups

3.1.2 Interaction with health and safety legislation

Economic incentives could be applied in such a way that they offer a powerful supplement to health and safety regulation.

As mentioned in the Introduction (Section 1.3) the incentives we propose here have been designed to promote additional efforts beyond those demanded by legislation. This implies a division of labour and responsibility with the health and safety authorities, since the general aim of improving the working environment coincides. The rationale for such a division is especially clear when the incentives form part of governmental/legislative activity. In that case it is difficult to imagine authorities rewarding enterprises for moving from an illegal to a legal working environment. As we shall demonstrate below, however, incentives may be used to do just that.

If we assume for the moment that incentive methods are related to additional efforts beyond those required by legislation, this poses the problem of identifying the level required by legislation. In most European countries the standards of working environment expected are flexible within limits. There is a spectrum of compliance:

○ Some matters can clearly be considered illegal and below the standard required by law.

○ Some aspects of the working environment are subject to judgment by public officers or bodies such as:
  – the labour/factory inspector
  – the labour/factory inspectorate at a local level
  – the labour/factory inspectorate at a central level
  – the courts.

Some of these judgments would be contentious if they were subject to public examination.

○ Some aspects of the working environment can clearly be demonstrated to be beyond the legislative requirements.

Furthermore, as the problems of the working environment evolve so the law will have to change dynamically.

The relationship between health and safety legislation and the economic incentive scheme could take these conclusions into consideration by:

1. A rule that no reduction or bonus can be given to an enterprise if the health and safety authorities have issued a mandatory command or otherwise signalled suspicion of illegality against the enterprise. This could be extended to include other disputes the enterprise might be involved in such as workers' formal complaints related to working environment, and external environment problems. It could apply to the enterprise as a whole even though it might be just one department that has received warning from the health and safety authorities.

2. Organising close co-operation between the EMMI-body and the authorities responsible for the health and safety legislation. There is an element of judgment that cannot be avoided and therefore predisposes to an organisational solution. Therefore the health and safety authority should decide the question of compliance. It needs to have a veto and the authority to delay proposals from the insurance body. This subject is elaborated in Section 5, Organisation.

3. Relating the most powerful bonus and the deepest premium reductions to efforts that are clearly beyond the requirements of legislation. Also possible by relating smaller bonuses to the higher end of the legal spectrum; efforts here represent a little more than just good practice.

The relationship between the law and the reductions obtainable is sketched in Figure 1.

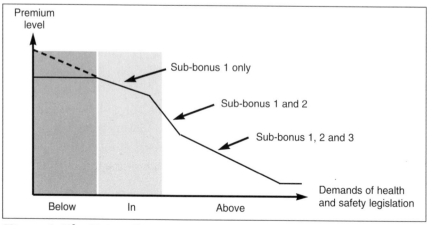

Figure 1: The Bonus Curve

4. The enterprises with working environments which are below or on the border of legality are assigned the highest level of premium, (indicated by the horizontal line in the figure), thus giving them an incentive to move towards a better working environment and compliance with the law. Furthermore the option of augmenting the premium paid to EMMI, when an illegally operating company is found by the health and safety authorities or by the EMMI-body, remains open (indicated by the sloping line in the figure).

5. Finally, consideration could be given to co-ordinating sanctions towards illegally acting enterprises, which continue to act illegally. This situation could be handled by a joint effort of the health and safety authorities and the EMMI-body.

3.2 Premium Graduation

The premium for an enterprise reflects the total risk of occupational injuries for that enterprise. Graduation is used to reflect different risk levels in different sectors and work processes. Furthermore, the graduation is used to reflect assessed and predicted future augmentations of the total risk as well as the risks currently experienced. The premium will rise if the total predicted risk is rising.

> **Premium**
> The term "premium" is used as a generic description for the sum paid to the EMMI-body independent of the organisation of this body (public, association, private or other).

Thus, enterprises are paying for the presence of specific risks in the workplace. This is the central incentive since it covers all enterprises. The incentive lies, apart from the bonus possibilities, in the fact that new risks are continuously included in the evaluation of the enterprise. The basis of evaluation will include experience, future risks and classification of enterprises. It is further elaborated in Section 4, together with the method of documentation.

If it is desired to prevent future injuries it is necessary to let the premium reflect the risk of these future injuries, without certain knowledge about whether or not the injuries will actually occur.

The gross premium, which is the highest level of premium and assigned to enterprises with the highest assessed risk, can be derived from three components:

○ The **base component** covers the aspect of joint and several liability ("solidarity") and administration expenses.

○ The **sector-related component** is needed because production processes, technology and organisation are central determinants of the risk.

○ The **work function-related component** reflects the fact that the risk of injuries is related to the actual jobs involved.

The partition of the three components is roughly 10%, 30% and 60%.

Base (solidarity)	Sector and Size of Enterprise	Work functions
(app.10%)	(app.30%)	(app.60%)

Figure 2: Elements of the gross premium

3.2.1 The base component

The actual costs of an accident can vary almost at random. Compare for example a young person without a family who dies, in contrast to the mother of a family who is disabled for life. Both could easily be the actual consequence of "one" risk. The joint and several liability element of the base component is that part of the premium which equalises these huge differences in risk. Joint and several liability ensures that differences in risk and the impact of coincidence are mediated.

In addition, there is an administrative contribution which means that the expenses for and administration of a payment system are shared. This component of the premium can only be influenced by the establishment of an efficient and administratively simple system.

3.2.2 The sector and enterprise size component

This element reflects the general occupational injury risk connected with the sector of industry and size of enterprise. This means that solidarity will exist within a specific sector, covering the risks in the sector which are so general that they can only be affected by the sector through joint action. Certain risks, for instance, can only be eliminated through the development of totally new production methods, or if the use of specific substances and materials is generally abandoned.

> **Concerted action by a sector**
> In Denmark, the consensus on the risk of brain damage from solvents in paints has resulted in the entire painting sector advocating the development of good, water-borne paints and gradually shifting to using only such paints in their production.

The motivating element to change this part of the premium lies at sector level rather than at the individual enterprise level. However, this part of the premium for an individual enterprise may be influenced if somehow the enterprise has reached an individual solution which deviates positively from the general occupational injury risk in the sector concerned.

3.2.3 The work function component

The actual occupational injury risk is closely related to *work functions*, i.e. the tasks actually conducted. Work with cutting tools and machinery, for instance, leads to many open wounds and amputations whereas work with substances and materials gives rise to brain damage, skin diseases and lung diseases. Processes and materials are thus key determinants of the type of risk involved in the work and of the preventive action needed to eliminate that risk.

The work function component must reflect the maximum risk known for occupational injuries in respect of the work function concerned, since enterprises which have arranged their work functions in a better way can then achieve a reduction in premium through the bonus system.

The premium can thus be influenced by the individual enterprise since the enterprise can arrange the workplace and organise the work in such a way that the actual risk is less than the maximum known risk.

As a starting point the gross-premium should be determined by the highest risk level for the sector and size of enterprise as well as by the work functions involved. The goal is to make it attractive for as many enterprises as possible to obtain a bonus. To do so, the enterprises should be able to prove that they provide a good working environment which as a minimum meets their obligations under legislation.

3.3 The bonus system

The technological development of a sector often leads to the generation of common hazards. This in turn may lead to the development of preventive actions and attempts at solutions that are widely applicable across a sector or for a particular work function across different sectors.

Hence, a bonus can be given to encourage such efforts. *The bonus is a reduction of the premium.* The efforts can cover a variety of investments and activities all designed to lead to a reduced risk. Some examples are given in the Box on page 46.

The procedure is to start out by setting a gross premium and then to consider what level of bonus (i.e. discount) might be possible. This might mean that only a few enterprises pay the gross premium without any reduction.

It follows from the discussion in Section 2 that the system should aim at achieving **uniform conditions**: enterprises with the same level of risk should pay the same rate. If several insurance bodies are acting, their premium and evaluation methods should be unified (see Section 4).

Augmentation and reduction of the premium should be limited. It is recommended that small enterprises with less than 50 employees should not suffer a rise in the rate greater than 100%. The exception to this is when the rise is part of a sanction.

The bonus can be composed of elements, or **sub-bonuses**, which are related to the different components of the overall premium and are offered in return for different types of effort (see Figure 1 on Page 41):

EXAMPLES OF EFFORTS LEADING TO A BONUS

The crucial criterion is that the effort should be greater than that demanded by legislation. In each of the examples it is assumed that the required standards (such as tools for handling heavy loads or machine guarding in accordance with European standards) have already been achieved. They should be understood as illustrative only since legislation varies from country to country.

Technical efforts:

* Extraordinary safety equipment on new machinery.
* Tripling safety systems in machine design instead of doubling.
* Innovation of new chemical substances to permit substitution.

Organisational efforts:

* Rearranging work procedures so that heavy loads can always be handled by double manning.

Training and education efforts:

* Additional health and safety education to health and safety representatives.
* Additional health and safety education to broad groups of employees.

Sub-Bonus 1 For universally specified efforts. The bonus rewards enterprises which have already made an effort in comparison to their competitors and can be obtained without the enterprise having to submit a special application.

Sub-Bonus 2 For generically specified efforts related to the shared problems of a sector or type of work. The bonus is given when the enterprise applies and is intended to stimulate industry to further specific actions.

Sub-Bonus 3 For an individually specified innovative effort related to the specific problems of an enterprise or organisation.

Each of these is described further below:

Sub-Bonus 1 - a general bonus

The purpose of Sub-Bonus 1 is to reduce the share of the base component of the gross premium which is determined by the work function element. The idea is to prompt the enterprise to assess the actual risk in the workplace and make changes so that the work functions involve fewer risk factors than are fixed in the gross premium.

This bonus can in principle be given without an application by the enterprise. The minimum level of bonus could be 10% of the gross premium.

The benefits of this type of sub-bonus are:-

1. To fix the premium level on the basis of a current risk assessment.

2. To have an opportunity of indicating to the individual enterprise the fields in which it is doing well and in which areas additional bonus can be obtained if further preventive action is taken.

3. That it will be simple to adjust the bonus when new initiatives have been carried through, since the gross premium and Sub-Bonus 1 together will always reflect the current risk, i.e. an investment in an enterprise may release a bonus immediately and thus illustrate the connection between action and return which constitutes an important motivational link.

4. This type of bonus targets all sizes of enterprises: small, medium-sized and large.

Sub-Bonus 2 - a bonus for specified efforts

The purpose of Sub-Bonus 2 is to consider preventive initiatives of a specified nature which it is desired either to give particularly high priority or which have not been considered through Sub-Bonus 1. There might be, say, five specified efforts per sector. One example might be the establishment of a safety circle.

Safety circles

A safety circle is often organised as regular meetings of representatives from management and employees from different parts of the enterprise. The agenda for the meetings can be informal and the idea is to make public all kinds of small and large working environment problems. Cross-company circles may be organised for small firms.

Safety circles have been developed from quality circles and have proven their utility in several investigations and in extensive practice in some countries and companies. Though there is no simple connection between the implementation of safety circles and risk, all studies agree that the probability of accidents (and sickness, in the case of health circles) was reduced. The costs of these circles are pretty high, because the sessions need the total participation of the staff, have to be carried out in small groups with a trained moderator and have to be repeated to be effective.

Since safety circles are, to the best of our knowledge, voluntary in all EU member states, they are a real extra in the field of safety training and instruction. They are an organisational measure promotable by the incentive scheme.

Sub-Bonus 2 will influence the sector element of the gross premium and the work function component depending on the nature of the initiatives.

The specification of the efforts related to Sub-Bonus 2 is done by co-operation between the EMMI-body and the social partners in a sector (see Section 5). This is to ensure that targets with a politically high priority are selected.

Generally, Sub-Bonus 2 will only be considered upon written request by the individual enterprise which itself is obliged to document that a specified effort has been made.

The written request is however intended to be simple since the enterprise only has to refer to what specified effort it has made. The application might be a standard form. Thus it should be reasonably practicable even for small enterprises to make the effort and apply for it.

The benefits of this type of sub-bonus are that:

1. Motivation is achieved towards specified preventive initiatives reaching beyond the framework of legislation.

2 Enterprises are encouraged to consider the whole risk rather than details.

3. A bonus can be granted for more general efforts which have an effect on the safety of the employees across all the work functions of an enterprise.

4. The parties of the sector are involved in the fixing of the bonus and are thus further motivated.

5. The bonus targets all sizes of enterprises; small, medium-sized and large.

Sub-Bonus 3 - a bonus for individual efforts

The purpose of Sub-Bonus 3 is to consider the enterprise that deviates materially as far as risk is concerned from other enterprises in the same sector or size group. Enterprises are grouped into sectors according to the products or the services on which their business is based. From the working environment angle, the production methods applied in a particular enterprise may distinguish themselves so much from the general characteristics of the sector that it will be necessary to make an individual evaluation of the enterprise and/or special work functions within the individual enterprise.

The initiative to make such an individual evaluation lies with the individual enterprise.

The benefits of this type of sub-bonus are, in addition to those mentioned under Sub-Bonus 2, that enterprises experiencing special problems or wishing to be in the forefront of their sector can receive financial compensation for their effort.

The drawback is that small enterprises may be resistant to the paperwork necessary to obtain this kind of bonus. It will need external assistance and this limits the number of small companies participating.

3.4 Special scheme for small enterprises

The special scheme for small enterprises should bridge the gap between the incentives offered in the general scheme and the particular way that small enterprises operate.

Small enterprises are assumed to have more or less the same health and safety problems as larger companies in the sector they belong to, but less internal manpower to deal with the transformation of the incentives.

Hence it is proposed that the scheme funds the employment of **prevention consultants**. They would have the task of promoting preventive action in a group of small enterprises. One example might be thirty small enterprises in the same geographic region operating in the same sector. Another could be a geographically more concentrated group of enterprises in different sectors (say situated in the same street). In either case it might be necessary to incorporate safeguards to prevent disclosure of confidential information which could affect competition between the participating enterprises.

The consultants' promotion of preventive action could take its point of departure in the specific problems of the participating enterprises. The consultants could be **authorized to propose the design of specific incentives**. This could for example be the establishing of a cross-company safety circle. When designing specific efforts the consultant can utilize the incentive scheme to help the enterprise obtain bonuses and investment aid if necessary.

Central to the success of this activity will be the development of mutual confidence between the consultant and the social parties of the enterprises.

The funding from the EMMI-body might cover, say, 50% of the expenses of the prevention consultant; the rest would be covered by the participating enterprises.

The preventive actions should aim at bringing the working environment of the enterprise above the standard required by health and safety law. It is therefore anticipated that the enterprises will obtain bonuses from the EMMI-body. These bonuses could be used to finance an enhancement of the prevention consultant scheme. This could be done if the scheme is more successful than the target set by the EMMI-body. The bonuses earned could be withheld until the EMMI-body's proportion of the prevention consultants' fees is paid.

The prevention consultants could be recruited from enterprises or from professional health and safety groups and be trained by the EMMI-body.

In some countries local resource centres (such as the Italian occupational health service Unita Sanitaria Locale (USL)) might be a natural point of departure for the prevention consultant. In others the consultant could be working directly from one or several of the participating enterprises. In any case it is important to develop interprofessional exchange across sectors of experiences about health and safety problems and solutions.

Over and above this specific scheme the EMMI-body should pay particular attention to smaller enterprises. This could be achieved by devising an appropriate inspection and visit regime (see Section 5, Organisation).

3.5 Investment Aid

Investment aid is aimed at helping enterprises that want to achieve major changes incorporating preventive measures. Examples could include new technology, training efforts and product innovation. The need in this situation is a combination of know-how with available capital, especially risk capital. It is particularly appropriate to SME's (see Section 2.2.2).

The investment aid could be based on a contract describing the enterprise's proposed scheme, and could work as follows:

○   An evaluation is made of the risks connected with the major change. This evaluation is described in the next section.

○ The EMMI-body and the enterprise develop a schedule of investments and activities on the basis of the evaluation. This schedule should be followed by the enterprise.

○ A loan is given on terms more favourable than are available on the general market, which could mean lower interest rates and little or no security.

The loan provided may be limited to, say, 50% of the investment. Thus the enterprise would be motivated by its economic participation in the investment and the limited financial capability of the EMMI-body could be accommodated.

The interest on the loan could be significantly lower than general market terms during the implementation period described in the contract. On the other hand, if the demands of the contract are not met, it should be possible for the EMMI-body to augment the interest rate.

○ Control is by a detailed assessment of the enterprise made after the investments and activities are complete. The loan is turned into a grant if the scheme has been followed properly. If not, the EMMI-body should have the power to withdraw the loan.

3.6 Labelling for marketing

Some enterprises might like to gain a competitive edge by using their good working environment for advertising purposes. A label could be developed and issued by the EMMI-body to meet this need.

The label could be given for undertaking a specified effort that attains Sub-Bonus 2 or 3 in a particular year. Thus, the label would signify an effort above that required for compliance with health and safety legislation. This means that the label would recognise both a level of achievement and a process within the enterprise. It is hereby distinguished from the ISO 9000-series which is primarily concerned with process certification.

Enterprises wishing to apply for this label without attaining the bonus could apply for an audit financed by themselves.

In setting the criteria for such a label, it could be reserved as a mark of excellence by issuing it for a limited time period and by aiming to restrict it to about 25% of the enterprises in a sector.

3.7 Co-ordination with other incentives

Enterprises are motivated to improve health and safety by a number of different initiatives and organisations, including:

○ Public incentives for industrial development

○ Social security

○ Health and safety legislative bodies

○ Debates in employers' associations

○ Collective agreements made by employers' and employees' organisations.

The economic incentive of the EMMI-body can be **intensified** if it is coordinated with these other types of motivation. On the other hand many SME's are puzzled by the multiple possibilities of state funding which often has the result that the funds are not utilised!

The EMMI-body should therefore seek co-operation with other social institutions and agents. This can be done through

○ Joint campaigns

○ Joint support programmes (e.g. new technology designed to prevent risk)

○ Joint information material.

In some cases the EMMI-body might come across needs for **innovations** (such as new machines, materials, or training programmes) that go beyond what can be properly promoted by investment aid. In these cases co-operation with research councils or other government science-promoting units is necessary. It is not possible to draw a firm line between what can be promoted by this incentive and what should be promoted by research funding. This is dependent on the enterprise and supplier involved. If the supplier of a given innovation is interested in developing a safer technology because of a presumed market it is possible to obtain results even within the investment aid framework.

A more formalised system of co-operation should be established between the EMMI-body and the **health and safety authorities**. This co-operation could ensure exchange of experiences in a broad way, and also provide a forum to discuss new generically specified bonus efforts. The health and safety authority could have a rôle in approving these new efforts.

Documentation and Evaluation

4

This section starts by describing the basic data needed for risk calculations and then goes on to describe how to use the data for evaluations in the proposed incentive methods.

4.1 Basic data and statistics

It is necessary to use past experience of the working environment for risk calculations, particularly for the premium graduation model. The goal is to extract as much knowledge as possible from this experience and then utilise the knowledge to predict the current risk of future injuries.

To this experience must be added new knowledge of risks that emerges from working environment studies, inspection visits, reports from enterprises, occupational medicine research and the like. This new knowledge gives rise to a re-evaluation of the existing risks which can be augmented or reduced, and it may lead to new risks being incorporated in the calculations.

It is this re-evaluation which, converted into an increase or reduction of the premium, creates the central incentive of the gross premium.

The information required to enable us to do the risk evaluations and the calculations includes a number of fundamental statistics together with the continuous documentation and observation of research projects. In particular the following areas will be discussed:

○ Information about the consequences of risks in the work environment.

○ Information about workforces and companies.

○ Information about the actual work environment.

○ Information about the causes of risks and factors affecting risks.

The term "risk" in this connection relates to the risk of people incurring different types of injuries during work. These injuries comprise the following five categories:

○ *Occupational accidents*, i.e. injuries due to sudden and unexpected events.

○ *Occupational diseases*, i.e. illness and injuries due to long-term exposures from the working environment.

○ *Other acute injuries*, i.e. acute injuries caused by exposures from the working environment for a short or long period of time which therefore cannot be characterised as an accident.

○ *Attrition*, i.e. diseases caused by particularly stressful work for a long period of time which are not generally accepted as obvious occupational diseases, but which nevertheless invoke disablement pensions, voluntary early retirement pensions, or the like.

○ *Other nuisances* resulting in frequent absence due to illness or medical treatment.

4.1.1 Information about consequences of risks

All types of injuries including occupational accidents and diseases which arise as a result of poor working environments should be registered.

○ The frequencies of injuries should be classified according to:

- Information about the injured person including profession, work function, age, sex and type of injury.
- Information about the company in which the injury occurred including industry classification, number of employees and type of production.

○ Severity of injuries should be classified by:
- Information about the injuries including financial, medical, occupational and social consequences.

○ Patterns of cause of the injuries should be classified by:
- Information about exposures and types of incidents in relationship to the work function in which the injury happened and the consequences it resulted in.

Ongoing registration of occupational accidents reported by employers and occupational diseases reported by doctors can generate such statistics. Registers of invalidity pensions, hospitalizations, sick pay, cause of death etc. can also be essential sources for identifying the consequences of poor working environments.

Types of injuries

Risk calculations require knowledge of the frequency of injuries within the relevant categories, and weighting of the severity of the individual types of injuries. The types of injuries to be considered are presented in Table 3.

The severity of injuries

Serious injuries could be given greater weight than less serious injuries; however, it is difficult to quantify the severity of injuries. The following possible methods of quantification are proposed:

○ Years lost

○ Number of sickness days/lost working days

○ The costs connected with hospital treatment, medical treatment, medicine, rehabilitation and possible compensation

○ A medical assessment of the degree of disablement/degree of inability to work.

TYPES OF INJURIES	
Accidents	**Occupational Diseases**[*]
Death	Infectious diseases
Amputation	Cancer
Bone fracture	Blood diseases and metabolic disorder
Sprains	
Open wounds	Mental illness
Heat-induced injuries	Diseases of the nervous system and the sensory organs
Cold-induced injuries	
Hearing damage	Brain damage diagnoses
Injuries from blows or shoves	Diseases of the circulatory system
Caustic injuries	Respiratory diseases
Poisoning	Allergies
	Gastrointestinal diseases
	Urogenital diseases
	Pregnancy diseases & children's diseases
	Skin diseases
	Diseases of the motor system
	Traumas and toxic injuries

[*] ICD-9 classification headings (International Classification of Diseases, WHO, Geneva).

It is important to make sure that all injuries are weighted as major or minor, which means that judgments are necessary in some cases. This is for instance the case with injuries leading to death which are given a high weight although no sickness days, expenses for treatment or disablement are involved.

Moreover, it may be necessary to subdivide the types of injuries into smaller groups according to the part of the body concerned, e.g. eye, shoulder, arm, wrist, hand, fingers, hip joint, leg, ankle, foot, toes.

Causes or exposure factors

The causes or exposure factors to focus on can be summarised as:

○ hazardous exposures that result in accidents and immediate injuries. These may be divided according to the type of energy involved;

○ hazardous exposures which after a long or short period, have resulted in injuries or are judged likely to result in injuries in the future;

○ the factors at individual workplaces which influence the degree to which individual exposures affect the individual human being and thus determine whether injuries arise.

Suggested classifications for these elements are given in the three following boxes.

Causes of immediate injuries

○ Energy which cuts, divides or planes, which is usually connected with various types of sharp objects such as knives, saws, edges etc.

○ Energy which presses and compresses which is usually connected with various types of moulding processes such as presses or with assembly tools.

○ Energy where kinetic energy is transformed into potential energy by something that moves, hits, knocks against or falls towards the human being.

○ Energy where potential energy in the human being is transformed into kinetic energy, as in the case of a fall from one level to another.

○ Energy in the form of heat/cold.

○ Energy in the form of electricity.

○ Energy in the form of acutely toxic or caustic substances.

○ Energy in the form of acute exposure to sound, light, radiation or vibrations.

○ Energy which strains the body excessively such as heavy weights, twisting, etc.

○ Energy straining the psyche excessively such as violence or threats of violence.

Hazardous exposures

○ Physical exposures such as noise, radiation, cold/heat, lighting, etc.

○ Psychological exposures such as work in isolation, monotony, threats, etc.

○ Physiological exposures, such as heavy burdens, repetitive work, inexpedient work postures, etc.

○ Chemical exposures, such as solvents, dust, asbestos, quartz, toxic substances, etc.

○ Biological exposures, such as animal hair, blood, viruses, bacteria, etc.

Exposure factors

○ The layout of the work space with a view to whether the person comes into contact with the harmful exposures.

○ The intensity of the exposure and the time during which the person is exposed to the risk.

○ How enclosed the work processes are and their maintenance so as to avoid errors and unplanned exposures.

○ How organised the work and the work conditions are so as not to lead to inexpedient actions or exposures.

○ The extent to which safety and health have been considered in connection with the organisation of work and general planning by the enterprise.

○ The extent to which training has been given in execution of the work to ensure safe and healthy conduct by the individual human being.

4.1.2 Information about workforces and enterprises

The workforce and its tasks should be registered as well as the enterprises and their production.

The registration and subsequent statistical analysis must cover:

○ The number of employees, classified by
  - occupations
  - work functions
  - age and sex
  - types of business (industry)
  - sizes of companies.
○ The number of enterprises classified by
  - sector
  - size (with information about the number employed and their work functions).

It is essential to make sure that the information in the different registration systems is collected according to the same principles and classifications so that comparisons and calculations of incidence rates are possible.

Occupations and work functions

Different types of work involve different types of risks. To be able to evaluate this, a classification of the human work activities at the enterprises is necessary. From experience, job titles and trade groups are too general and do not sufficiently reflect shared tasks and/or risks. Conversely, the classification must be practicable and therefore not too detailed. Here, we use the work function concept to describe a group of tasks at the enterprise with appreciable shared characteristics as regards the use of tools, technology and working environment. A typical production facility can for instance be divided into seven work function categories:

○ Production functions
○ Transport functions
○ Maintenance and repair functions
○ Administrative functions
○ Warehouse functions
○ Cleaning functions
○ Canteen functions.

Work function groupings can be defined on the basis of international classifications used for data collection on employment and occupational accidents. The ISCO classification (International Standard Classification of Occupations, ILO, Geneva) could be used as a starting point. It divides occupational groups hierarchically i.e. first into major groups, then into sub-groups etc. The Box following shows the first level ISCO codes, but it could be decided analytically at which level the ISCO classification is to be used.

ISCO Classification - Major groups
1   Legislators, senior officials and managers
2   Professionals
3   Technicians and associate professionals
4   Clerks
5   Service workers and shop and market sales workers
6   Skilled agricultural and fishery workers
7   Craft and related workers
8   Plant and machine operators and assemblers
9   Elementary occupations
0   Armed forces

Enterprises and sectors

The goal is to group industrial sectors into broader classes within which the enterprises can be viewed as comparable from a working environment point of view. At the same time, the groups should not be too small as regards the number of enterprises and number of employees.

The grouping of sectors and enterprise sizes proposed is based on an international classification. It is expedient to adopt a classification which is already used for collection of data on employment and the incidence of injuries as these data will form the basis of the calculations.

The grouping of sectors may thus follow the NACE classification (Nomenclature Statistique des Activités Économiques) based on two levels, e.g. NACE 1. digit and then on NACE 3. digit.

The division based on the size of the enterprises must be very crude, e.g.

- Small enterprises with less than 10 employees
- Enterprises with between 10 to 100 employees
- Large enterprises with between 100 to 1000 employees
- Group companies with more than 1000 employees.

The first level of the NACE code

A Agriculture, hunting and forestry
B Fishing
C Mining and quarrying
D Manufacturing
E Electricity, gas and water supply
F Construction
G Wholesale and retail trade; repair of motor vehicles, motorcycles and household goods
H Hotels and restaurants
I Transport, storage and communication
J Financial intermediation
K Real estate, renting and business activities
L Public administration and defence; compulsory social security
M Education
N Health and social work
O Other community, social and personal service activities
P Private households with employed persons
Q Extra-territorial organisations and bodies

If necessary this classification could be further divided into subsets to support, for example, a specific scheme for small enterprises.

4.1.3 Information about the actual work environment

The general risks and work environment factors that are actually present in different industries and work functions should be measured and registered.

This can be done through investigation of the industry and by making mapping studies as spot checks. Continuing measurements and workplace evaluations will also form the basis of knowledge about the standards of work environments.

The goal is to have an initial measure of the average position within a sector or a work function. A few companies should be compared with the average to see whether they are "good" or "bad".

This will also provide a baseline from which meaningful priority can be given to those efforts which should be able to earn a bonus. Furthermore the information gained could be used to develop guidance that would spur companies into action and improve the work environment independently of the other incentives.

4.1.4 Information about causes of risks and risk factors

Information about the causes of risks can be obtained from specific investigations, analyses and research.

Causes include sources of exposure to diseases, their duration, concentration and strength, synergistic effects etc. Medical and sociological investigations are the most important methods to illuminate this.

Causes also includes the factors which make accidents happen. Specific technical factors, organisational conditions and behaviour can all play a part. Technical and sociological investigations are the most important methods for demonstrating a connection.

Continuous follow-up is essential to check that incentives are effective. Monitoring should be designed to prevent accidents through a holistic approach to analysis, and should provide an additional source of knowledge about factors that affect risk.

4.2 Evaluation of premium graduation and bonus system

This section includes some suggestions on how to implement the proposed incentive methods. It deals with premium graduation and the bonus system as a combined method, whereas investment and the subsidy system are dealt with separately.

4.2.1 The gross premium

The base component

The base component is the part of the premium which compensates for random differences in risk and which covers the costs and administration of a payment system. It is named R_{base}.

The joint and several liability (solidarity) element is determined administratively, based on the system's general costs, and should only represent a minor share of the premium, e.g. 10%.

R_{base} can only be influenced by the establishment of an efficient and administratively simple system.

The sector/enterprise size component

The premium for the sector/enterprise size component can be fixed on the basis of statistical calculations of known risk, here defined as the current general injury frequency and severity. These calculations can be based on knowledge of what has happened historically within sectors and size classes. It is, however, important that the knowledge obtained from experience is corrected in the light of new research and changes in the production facilities, etc. which have either eliminated risks or/and created new ones.

The section on documentation requirements describes some proposals for the analysis and collection of data which are relevant to the completion of the calculations.

The risk is determined from the frequency of injuries, weighted according to their severity. Here, "injuries" means the five categories listed in the section on basic data, i.e. injuries due to accidents, injuries due to long-term exposure (occupational diseases), injuries caused by attrition, other acute injuries and nuisances resulting in absence due to illness and medical conditions. This component is named R_{sector}. The knowledge about risks that can be extracted from experience should only be taken into consideration when it relates to risks that still exist. Likewise new knowledge about new risks should be incorporated in risk assessment, even though the new risks have not yet resulted in injury claims.

The risk within each sector group must be analysed so that it is apparent which types of injuries are to be given the highest weight in the risk assessment. These should be the ones that will give the greatest benefit if the sector manages to prevent them.

Here, it is very important to use all the records available and to consider preventive measures already taken, thereby ensuring that the risk assessment is as up-to-date and generic as possible. It is also important that there is no incentive to lower the perceived risk by avoiding having the injuries reported.

The work function component

Different types of work involve different types of risks. As previously mentioned a typical production facility could for instance be divided into seven work function categories:

- Production functions
- Transport functions
- Maintenance and repair functions
- Administrative functions
- Warehouse functions
- Cleaning functions
- Canteen functions.

The work function element of the gross premium must reflect the maximum known risk of occupational accidents connected with that function since enterprises which have organised their work functions in a better way can then obtain a reduced premium through the bonus award.

The work function elements are calculated from statistics of known risks, here defined on the basis of expected general injury frequency and severity across sectors.

The calculations can be based on experience concerning injuries already incurred and other knowledge on the incidence of risk, e.g. from medical research. On this basis, a work function matrix indicating the maximum occupational injury frequency and the nature and severity of the injuries can be designed. Again the knowledge about risks that can be extracted from experience should only be taken into consideration when it relates to risks that still exist. Likewise new knowledge about new risks should be incorporated in the risk assessment, even though the new risks have not yet resulted in injury claims.

The list of work functions must be comparatively crude and only include a maximum of 10-20 options per sector group. It may be appropriate that where there is very little risk differentiation within the sector groups there should be very few work functions, whereas sectors with very high risk differentiation could be divided into more detailed work functions.

In this way it is possible to examine work functions which are carried out by few people in any individual enterprise, but which constitute a large high-risk group within the sector and/or within the whole labour force, e.g. cleaning, transport, etc. The work function element is defined as:

$R_{production}$
$R_{transport}$
$R_{administration}$

etc.

Procedure for setting the gross premium

The procedure for setting the gross premium is a combination of fixing the base element, the sector element and the work function element. Moreover, the premium will necessarily depend on the number of employees in the individual enterprise in terms of equivalent full-time man-years.

The fundamental idea is that each man-year/employee attracts a base amount, a sector amount and a work function amount. The base amount is the same for all employees in all sectors. The sector amount is the same for all employees in the individual sector but varies for employees from different sectors. The work function amount is the same for all employees with the same work function, but varies for employees with different work functions.

An enterprise belonging to sector S employing N man-years with N consisting of A employees carrying out production functions, B employees carrying out administrative functions and C employees carrying out cleaning functions will attract a gross premium, made up as follows:

$$
\begin{aligned}
\text{Gross premium} = \quad & N \times R_{base} + \\
& N \times R_{sector} + \\
& A \times R_{production} + B \times R_{administrative} + C \times R_{cleaning}
\end{aligned}
$$

To fix the base premium for a real enterprise requires information on:

○ The sector to which the enterprise belongs

○ The number of employees at the enterprise on an annual basis

○ The distribution of the employees within various specified work functions.

It is also necessary to have available:

○ data on the general sector risk, R_{sector}

and

○ a work function matrix indicating the maximum known risk for the work functions, $R_{production}$, $R_{transport}$, R..............

Within the sector and work function groupings which are selected for calculation of risk levels, it is necessary to know the following:

$$
\begin{aligned}
\text{Current Risk} = \quad & \text{sum of the number of different types of injuries} \\
& \times \quad \text{severity of the injuries} \\
& \div \quad \text{the number of employees}
\end{aligned}
$$

The current risk may be calculated by combining the element of experience with an evaluation of future risks as follows:

○ First it is necessary to know the incidence rate for the different types of injuries, the nature of the injuries and the quantified consequences. In addition, the extent of the workforce - the number of persons - within the same sector and work function groupings must be known in order to calculate frequencies. This defines the experience element.

○ Second, the evaluation of future risks must be made. This means an evaluation of the significance of new knowledge, how it influences the various risks and the likely impact on the number of the various types of injuries.

To be able to evaluate the current risk in individual enterprises, in principle it is also necessary to know the cause-effect relationship for the different types of injuries. However, in practice some cause-effect correlations are not fully known and need to be supplemented by practical assessment.

4.2.2 The bonus system

The basic idea of the bonus system is to bring about a reduction of the calculated gross premium. Since the gross premium has been fixed at a high level based on a calculated maximum risk this means that a bonus may be given, i.e. a reduction of the gross premium, when it is shown that the actual risk is lower than the calculated one.

The actual risk in an enterprise can and often will differ from the calculated maximum risk both in relation to the sector to which the enterprise belongs and in relation to the work functions carried out at the enterprise. The difference between the calculated maximum risk and the actual risk assessed determines the extent of a bonus.

The bonus award may, for instance, vary in steps from 10% up to 50% of the gross premium for each of the sub-bonuses 1, 2 and 3.

Sub-Bonus 1 - a general bonus

This evaluation must be based on knowledge of the correlation between sources of exposure and risk of injury. Primarily the knowledge should come from completed written standard forms submitted by the enterprise. Additionally, evaluation should take place at inspection visits, with priority given to high-risk enterprises.

A job exposure matrix for the individual work functions should be prepared to enable a uniform evaluation to be made in an administratively simple way. This matrix must be a reference system stating the exposure sources that generally occur in individual work functions and the weight/influence they have on the incidence of occupational injuries. At the same time the matrix should indicate the effect of eliminating the exposure sources, or reducing them by different degrees, on the risk of occupational injury.

In order to minimise uncertainty of the evaluation and to simplify the system, five bonus levels are operated corresponding to a reduction of the risk connected with the work function element by 20, 40, 60, 80 and 100%, respectively.

The goal of the evaluation is to collect information on the current exposure incidence whereby the job exposure matrix provides the basis for calculation. This basis for calculation must be obtained from analyses of the causal relationship with the injuries that have arisen and through current working environment research.

Sub-Bonus 2 - for specified efforts

Possible initiatives may be of a technical, organisational or training nature. Initiatives should follow the principles indicated in Article 6.2 of the Framework Directive 89/391/EEC, viz.:

○ That the selected risks are completely eliminated e.g. by new production methods.
○ That the work is organised and arranged focusing on the individual.
○ That the working environment is organised based on the highest possible technical and social level.
○ That dangerous substances and materials are replaced by less dangerous substances and materials.
○ That solutions comprise an overall and co-ordinated whole for both technological, organisational, working environment and social relations.
○ That extraordinary training programmes are carried out.

At the same time, calculations must be made of the importance of the initiatives to the occupational injury risk and of their impact on the gross premium.

The bonus-earning initiatives could for instance be selected by advisers basing their choice on their own experience and available documentation. These advisers could come from different environments such as:

○ working environment professionals
○ sector professionals

- special incentives advisers
- trade associations
- unions with members in the sector.

It must be a precondition for bonus-earning initiatives that they must be easily identifiable while at the same time showing a clear correlation between the effort made and a measurable change of risk.

Bonus-earning initiatives could be selected based on the fact that they

- eliminate risks that involve serious consequences
- eliminate risks that give rise to frequent consequences
- eliminate risks that affect many employees
- eliminate or prevent exposure of the employees to risks
- help the employees with safe handling of risks.

If an enterprise makes a bonus-earning effort, this will affect its gross premium because the initiative will mean a change of R_{sector} as well as $R_{work\ function}$. Both risk factors will be changed due to the change in risk brought about by the initiative. However, only the $R_{work\ function}$ for those work functions affected by the initiative is influenced, which means that the bonus is only awarded in an amount proportional to the number of employees benefitting from the initiative.

In addition, a framework must be determined for a method to evaluate whether the initiatives have been followed and how many people the initiatives cover at the individual enterprise.

Generally, Sub-Bonus 2 will only be contemplated upon written request from the individual enterprise. The enterprise is responsible for documenting that a special effort has been made. Such documentation can subsequently be followed up by inspections or written feed-back depending on the nature of the initiatives and their implications on risk.

Sub-Bonus 3 - an individual bonus

The individual bonus is intended for enterprises which differ materially in production and/or organisation from other enterprises in the same sector. The enterprise might also have special work functions that differ materially from the traditional work functions of the sector in general.

Such enterprises cannot be evaluated on the same basis as the rest of the sector.

The individual bonus therefore represents an individual risk assessment as the more traditional method cannot be applied. Also, sufficient experience or documentation for a traditional risk calculation will probably not be available.

The initiative to make such an individual evaluation lies with the individual enterprise and will usually require an inspection of the enterprise and subsequent individual assessment.

The risk calculations in such individual cases must follow the same principles as those applying to the gross premium and in particular Sub-Bonus 1, i.e. they should be based on knowledge collected through the general statistics and documentation.

Evaluations will similarly have to be made of the extent of the occupational injury risk and the weight which the individual factors have on this. An evaluation could also be made of the number of employees who have been affected by the individual factors.

Sub-Bonus 3 requires an evaluation method and bonus award principles.

4.2.3 Organisation of the bonus system

It is the individual enterprise which must take the initiative to provide information or apply for a bonus award. Several different application methods can be used depending on the bonus type applied for.

Generally, the first step in a bonus award will be a written application. For Sub-Bonuses 1 and 2 the information will usually be given in tabular form. A more detailed description and review of the enterprise by specially trained inspectors/evaluation officers may have to be made later.

The enterprises can be divided into 3 categories, viz.

1. *High-risk enterprises* which will always require physical review and inspection by a special team of inspectors/evaluation officers.

2. *Medium-risk enterprises* which require inspection only in special cases or by spot checks. Elaborate descriptions completed by the Internal Safety Organisation at the enterprise or by the

Occupational Health Service, if any, will often provide a sufficient basis for evaluating the bonus potential.

3. *Low-risk enterprises* for which a possible bonus is usually decided on the basis of completed forms alone.

By dividing the enterprises into 3 risk levels the administrative procedure can be simplified significantly. In the case of high-risk enterprises it is necessary to carry out a resource intensive individual risk assessment. Medium-risk enterprises can be evaluated on the basis of written documentation combined with check inspections while low-risk enterprises can be administered in a more automatic fashion.

The criteria for bonus awards and calculation of risk functions R_{base}, R_{sector} and the $R_{work\ functions}$ must be determined centrally. Moreover, the safety and health conditions of importance to the individual bonus categories in the individual sector and work function must be clearly indicated.

When a gross premium has been fixed and a bonus possibly awarded, it should also be indicated which safety and health conditions the enterprise can subject to further improvements in order to obtain an additional bonus. This is the only way to clarify the correlation between an extra effort and extra financial gain.

4.3 Evaluation of investment aid

Investment aid depends on an evaluation of the change in risk which will be effected as a result of the investment. Usually, the investment will take place only in parts of the enterprise but in principle there ought to be no restrictions on this.

The focus in connection with investments will, on the face of it, be on technology and production facilities. However, organisational investments and investments in the training and education of staff beyond what is required by health and safety law are in fact quite as relevant. The essential factor is to provide improved safety and health conditions for the employees.

Evaluation of the actual risk at the enterprise prior to investment and evaluation of the lower risk expected after implementation can be made according to the same rules as those applying to the setting of the premium and the bonus award described in Section 4.2.

However, when considering investment aid, an actual evaluation of risk must be made through physical inspection by special inspectors/evaluation officers. The evaluation can be limited to that part of the enterprise in which the investment is to be made and similarly can be related solely to the number of employees who will be affected by the investment.

Deciding which eligible enterprises should have priority for investment aid, and when and for what purpose it should be given, depends on several factors such as:

○ investments solving high-risk problems, i.e. the risk of very serious injuries and/or frequent injuries.

○ investments resulting in improvements for a very large number of people.

○ investments leading to the development of radically new solutions improving safety and health.

○ investments that are particularly expensive for the enterprise seen in relation to the normal investment capability of the enterprise.

○ evaluation of economic stability.

4.4 Evaluation of labelling for marketing

As previously mentioned, labelling for marketing can be attached automatically to the bonus award. Therefore, no separate evaluation model is needed. We suggest that enterprises obtaining a 50% bonus be given a label, implying that they would have had to qualify for Sub-Bonuses 1, 2 and 3.

It is possible to specify other types of labelling rules. It is important, however, that they constitute a set of rules which is easy to understand, uniform across sectors and preferably also uniform across national borders.

Organisation

5

Following the detailed descriptions of the evaluation methods, this section discusses the organisation necessary to administer the economic incentive system, including conducting the evaluations. In other words, this section describes the EMMI-body.

The underlying assumption is that the incentive methods are relatively independent of the necessary organisation. This permits a number of alternative organisational structures which are discussed on several levels. It follows directly that these descriptions are of an advisory nature and have to be shaped to fit the context of the individual nation. It is assumed here that the whole scheme of incentive methods is implemented, but this, in practice, is subject to negotiation at the national level.

We will focus on the organisation necessary for the incentive methods, but we do touch the compensation side of the insurance system as well. It is generally assumed that the administration of workers' compensation is part of the same organisation.

In the next section we will discuss the actions that are necessary to implement the incentives scheme and the EMMI-body.

5.1 Demands on the organisation

The general demands on the organisation will be grouped as follows:

○ Separation of the income/incentive scheme from the expenses/workers compensation system

○ Cost effectiveness

○ Tasks to be conducted

○ Qualifications of the staff

○ Authorization

○ Co-operation with statutory health and safety authorities.

Each of these is discussed below.

The impact of the first demand, however, is that the discussion will be restricted to the incentive scheme part of the organisation.

5.1.1 Separation of incentive and compensation schemes

It is proposed to separate the two sides of the insurance body, economically and organisationally. The **income** side will include the incentive scheme and the **expense** side will include workers' compensation. It is assumed here that the EMMI-body is directly or indirectly part of a social-security system.

The principle for the compensation paid to injured people could be to assure them a good quality of life during recovery and/or after disablement. The compensation system could operate on the level of the societal development and so would be continually amended to include new diseases.

On the other hand the incentive scheme forms part of the overall task for the EMMI-body of collecting the necessary premiums. This should be done on the basis of accurate data about the actual and future risk for the individual enterprise. The basis of rating should be transparent for the enterprise (see below).

Hence the two sides have potentially conflicting aims and it is necessary to separate them in order to guarantee that the social security aspect and the legal rights of the compensation-claimer are maintained.

The EMMI-body with its tasks and incentive methods is assumed to be an independent economic system. It could be required to produce only a long term balance between compensation paid and premiums received. The economic balance could be achieved over the middle to long term (3-5 years). This could be done by establishing an alignment-fund. In the case of an adverse balance, the fund would support the incentive scheme account to the necessary extent and conversely the fund would receive any surplus produced.

Another reason for aiming at this long term balance is the element of chance in the severity and frequency of injuries, thus making short-term budgeting difficult.

The features of the alignment fund, the long term balance and the incorporation of future risks distinguish the EMMI system from the traditional "pay-as-you-go" system. It is, however, suggested that existing economic reserves be used to a limited extent to facilitate the transition to an EMMI system.

5.1.2 Cost effectiveness

The costs for administration and organisation should be held at a level which balances the opportunities from promoting prevention with the extra costs imposed on enterprises.

The expenses used for administration could be held as low as possible without affecting the prevention and compensation tasks. The organisation is intended to handle a major societal task and should therefore be dynamic and flexible. The organisation could use information technology and a skill-based and participatory management style. Quality management could be included. Education and training of employees could be compulsory. These criteria sketch some of the main elements of how to be cost-effective in a knowledge-based organisation like the EMMI-body.

Finally, administering low-risk enterprises in a technically simple way can be more efficient. Medium-risk enterprises can be administered through written documentation and check inspections, while high-risk enterprises primarily will demand more resources (see page 48).

5.1.3 Tasks to be conducted

The organisation should be able to carry out the following tasks:

○ Inspections and visits.

○ Monitoring - data collection: data on enterprises, employees, work functions, working environment, injury claims, investigations, surveys and other forms of new knowledge on the development of the working environment.

○ Rating/premium graduation.

○ Bonus setting.

○ Administration of complaints and appeals.

○ Sanctions; coping with enterprises acting illegally in relation to rating and/or the incentive scheme. (Illegality related to health and safety legislation is assumed to be dealt with elsewhere).

○ Generation and dissemination of information.

○ Co-ordinating efforts with other authorities.

○ Co-operation with the social partners.

Inspections and visits

Various kinds of inspections, interventions and visits at shop-floor level are central to several of the incentive methods. They are also important inputs to the information collection and monitoring activities. Therefore the organisation should be resourced with the necessary staff.

At the strategic level the EMMI-body could decide what aims should govern the inspection and visit activity:

○ Types of inspections, interventions and visits.

○ Targets for number of enterprises and frequency.

○ "Search and prioritize" - strategy.

○ Giving priority to small enterprises.

○ Quality criteria for the visits; expected results.

It is important to find the right balance between these aims. It is not necessarily a good idea to aim at a high number of visits. Rather the enterprises should be chosen carefully in order to obtain the greatest possible effect. This means visiting and working with high risk enterprises, but also picking cutting edge enterprises. These often offer a "window" on the rest of the sector.

Furthermore co-operation with the social partners of a branch can lead to enterprises wanting to be ahead of the field, thus creating a driving force for the rest of the sector.

It is assumed, however, that the implementation of the incentive methods outlined will lead to a higher number of visits than are conducted today by existing insurance bodies. The limitation of inspection visits to high-risk enterprises only will mean a reduction of resources spent on the evaluation.

Applying for Sub-Bonus 3 or for investment aid will involve intensive visits including workplace inspection and the negotiation of terms. Other types of interventions include sanctions as described below.

Administration of complaints and appeals

The enterprises could have the option to appeal against the evaluation and ratings made by the EMMI-body. The appeals may range from the number of employees registered to disagreement on investment aid contracts.

An appeal board independent of the EMMI-body could be the second authority involved.

This system of complaints and appeals is intended to ensure a just procedure from the EMMI-body. It could designed, however, in a way that also avoids the misuse of complaints and appeals by enterprises. In general this could be done by letting the judgment of the EMMI-body stand until the appeal board has pronounced.

Sanctions/Coping with Breach of Contract

Sanctions are defined as actions taken against enterprises which act in direct opposition to the preventive aims of the incentive scheme.

This occurs if, for example:

- Enterprises deliberately falsify information on their internal conditions.
- Enterprises misuse risk capital given to them as part of the investment aid.
- The marketing label is abused.
- Enterprises deliberately apply for a bonus without making the specified effort.
- Enterprises notify too few employees to the EMMI-body.

On the other hand, introducing hazardous processes or breaking health and safety regulations in other ways is not part of the EMMI-body's sanction scheme. Such matters should in principle be controlled by other authorities.

Breaches made by enterprises and discovered by the insurance body could be evaluated by the body. It could be made possible for the EMMI-body to prescribe criteria for the gravity of infringements and to have authority to let minor violations pass without further action (a *threshold limit for trivia*).

A sanctions procedure could start with several attempts to establish dialogue with the enterprise. This could take the form of visits or other communications with an advisory tone and comprising dialogue with the social partners of the enterprise. This could be tried for a specified period of time.

The next step could be to impose a sanction in form of an augmented premium. This procedure could be followed if necessary by further augmentations over time and depending on the seriousness of the offence.

The possibility of public justice being imposed in grave cases could be incorporated in the insurance contract. The contract conditions may be issued as part of legislation so that a breach would be an offence that could be publicly prosecuted.

Sanctions are considered an exceptional incentive method. They are used only when other forms of dialogues with an enterprise prove insufficient.

5.1.4 Qualifications of the staff

The conduct of the tasks outlined demands a specific pattern of qualifications for the staff as a whole including:

- Health and safety competence:
  - knowledge of risk factors
  - ability to solve health and safety problems
- Knowledge of health and safety legislation
- Economic and statistical competence:
  - risk calculation, rating assessment, realization of joint and several liability
- Developing a new multi-skilled competence:
  - understanding the enterprise as a social system and the patterns of reaction when economically motivated
  - intervention techniques and follow up (e.g. coping with organisational change)
- Use of information technology.

The organisation could recruit and train people to meet these demands. This question is discussed further in Section 6.

5.1.5 Authorization

The EMMI-body could operate within a legal framework that allows it to act as an insurance company for the enterprises. This authorization could also include a description of accepted sanctions as well as the basic requirements for an insurance contract.

5.1.6 Co-operation with legal health and safety authorities

It is crucial for the proper functioning of the incentive scheme that it is closely co-ordinated with health and safety authorities. This co-ordination could cover a series of topics, such as:

- A joint procedure for the recognition of bonus criteria.
- A joint procedure for co-operation with the social partners of the industrial sectors.
- Exchange of experience and shared use of monitoring data.
- Common training of employees within the EMMI-body and the health and safety authorities.

The joint procedures for developing and recognising bonus criteria could build on, among other sources, statistical material provided by the health and safety authorities as well as the EMMI-body. When arranging the data on health and safety by sectors it is possible to develop a chart of the situation in each sector, thus creating a basis for the consideration of new bonuses. Therefore joint work on the standards for monitoring data, with compatible statistics and information technology, is crucial.

Exchange of experience could be a tool for constantly developing the understanding of new health and safety problems in industry and elements of solutions applied in practice. The exchange could be organised on a regional or sectoral level. It could combine the experiences of factory inspectors from the health and safety authorities with the experiences of employees in the EMMI-body who are working, for example, on the evaluation of bonus applications.

This co-operation could be further enhanced by joint campaigning on issues of mutual interest: prevention of specific types of accidents, training of safety personnel, etc.

5.1.7 Co-operation with the social partners

The realization of the incentive scheme outlined could be viewed as a major societal task. The viewpoint taken here is that achieving such a task necessitates the active involvement of the social partners at all levels; enterprise, sector, region and society. The social partners are to be viewed as a critical resource.

At the enterprise level the transformation of the push from the incentive scheme into prevention activities is wholly dependent on the partners in the enterprise, that is the workers, worker representatives, engineers, clerks, lower level management and top management.

All kinds of activities stemming from the EMMI-body should reflect this. The employer could be obliged to inform all partners of the premium paid and the changes to the premium; or the EMMI-body could carry the obligation to inform all parties, for example by a system of contact persons.

Inspections and visits could be designed in a way that secures the full involvement of all partners in the visits as well as in the evaluation of the results.

The **design of the specified efforts related to Sub-Bonus 2** implies co-operation with the social partners of the industrial sectors at sector level and regional or societal level.

When the design is done jointly the motivation of the partners represents an extra driving force behind the scheme. The day to day practical knowledge of the partners, and also their political programmes, could be integrated into the efforts planned. On the other hand the professional viewpoint of the EMMI-body could also play a major role.

A balance could be achieved through the procedure applied for the specification of efforts:

○ The status of major health and safety issues in the sector as well as proposals for the efforts should be detailed by the EMMI-body.

○ The social partners of the branch could participate in the decision on which efforts should be promoted in a given period (related to Sub-Bonus 2). This participation could be on an advisory level or at a more "responsible" level involving decision-making. The latter implies greater motivation by the social parties.

If the social partners cannot agree on which efforts to initiate, the EMMI-body should try to formulate a compromise and should act as mediator. If the mediation fails the EMMI-body should have the final say in which efforts to initiate.

5.2 Organisational models

In this section possible organisational models are discussed. It is assumed that the organisation as a whole is responsible for the income/incentive scheme as well as the expenses/compensensation side. The overall focus is, however, on the income side.

Common questions which must be answered include:

○ How can the model accomplish the necessary tasks?

○ How is prevention enforced?

○ How can economy and effectiveness be ensured?

○ What is the relationship to the Third Insurance Directive (92/49/EEC)?

○ How can the system achieve a clear-cut distinction between the incentive and compensation sides of the EMMI-body?

Directive 92/49/EEC

The Third Insurance Directive regulates the competition in the insurance market as part of the European free internal market. It prohibits Member States from creating legislation controlling the operation of insurance companies. Furthermore the Directive aims to allow insurance companies freedom of operation in all EU countries. Hence any workers' compensation insurance organised on the basis of private enterprise is affected and any insurance company could undertake such business in any country.

The Directive also sets standards for economic reserves etc.

5.2.1 State institution

This model implies positioning the organisation inside the state system, thus transforming the premiums into a form of tax. The body described would have a monopoly on insurance.

The outline of the incentive method relates to elements of government policy on industrial development, social security and the labour market including health and safety. Hence a state model necessitates firstly a decision on which ministry should be responsible. Secondly it needs a strong co-ordination effort since these three policy areas normally are split between three ministries.

There is also a need for strong co-ordination with the health and safety authorities. The risk of rivalry with the authorities is considerable. This remains true even if the EMMI-body is placed under the auspices of the same ministry but in a separate organisation.

The model implies a unified system with uniform conditions for enterprises. Furthermore it implies good cost-effectiveness related to the standardisation of large-scale administrative procedures.

The model does not conflict with the Third Insurance Directive.

The possibilities of achieving clear-cut distinction between incentives and compensation sides of the EMMI-body are quite good. The separation necessitates as a minimum two sub-organisations with different management and budgets, but the two sides of the body could even be located in two different ministries.

5.2.2 Independent institution

The independent organisation could be authorized by law to be responsible for the incentive method as well as for the compensation system as a whole. It would thus be a monopoly.

It could be managed by the social partners or be constituted as an association with social partners in a more advisory role.

The model implies a unified system with uniform conditions for enterprises. Furthermore it implies good cost-effectiveness related to the standardisation of large scale administrative procedures.

The independence from the state system might create too business-oriented a management style. This contradicts the overall societal aims of the system (such as creating a good standard of living for injured people and not having to do short term balanced accounts). On the other hand, some of the management aims might be supported better in such an organisation.

Co-ordination with ministries and the health and safety authorities is crucial. If the co-ordination is too weak it might create rivalry.

The Third Insurance Directive might create problems for such an institution.

It would be more complicated to achieve clear-cut separation between the incentive and compensation sides of the EMMI-body than in the "state model". The separation necessitates as a minimum two sub-organisations with different management and budgets. The two sides of the body could, however, be situated in two independent organisations within two different ministries.

5.2.3 Controlled private organisation

The controlled private organisation is a private company authorized by law to be responsible for the incentives as well as workers' compensation. It would thus have a monopoly as the independent organisation. It could be managed as a private enterprise and still co-operate with the social partners and the authorities.

The organisation would be able to create a uniform system with uniform conditions for enterprises. It could, however, due to the Third Insurance Directive, not be obliged to do so by law.

The independence from the state system might create a business-like concern for turnover in contrast to the social security aspects of the compensation system. Furthermore this company might assess risks differently to a state system.

Co-ordination with ministries and the health and safety authorities would be crucial. If the co-ordination were weak, commercial values might be stressed at the expense of societal values. Furthermore it might create rivalry.

It would be more complicated to create clear-cut separation between the incentive and the compensation sides of the EMMI-body. The overall system could be subordinated to short-term economic considerations.

5.2.4 Total private

In this model the EMMI-body comprises private insurance companies that compete with each other. This implies a **non-unified system** since each company might chose its own premium policy. One possibility might be to bundle the injury insurance with other kinds of insurance.

The possible cost-effectiveness of large scale operation is replaced by the forces of competition, which create a contradiction to the societal aims. It becomes very difficult to achieve the strong co-ordination needed, and the risk of rivalry with the health and safety authorities is considerable.

Furthermore it is impossible to prescribe a specific model for incentives or premium assessment. It is likely that the companies will make their own assessments on the basis of evaluation of their own risks, which will be different to the risks assessed from society's viewpoint.

The Third Insurance Directive might create problems for such organisations, and might also interfere with the creation of "framework" laws by governments.

The possibilities of achieving clear-cut separation between the incentive and compensation sides of the EMMI-body are complicated and probably not cost-efficient. The two sides of the body would have to exist within each active company.

5.2.5 Mixed models

The mixing of the above three main models can be done in different ways: coupling all three together, two of them, or even a three body model. Some major examples might be:

○　The state co-ordinates with private insurance companies.
○　The state co-ordinates with an independent institution.
○　An independent institution co-ordinates with private insurance companies.

The boundaries of responsibilities between these organisations need to be carefully considered. Even so there is considerable need for co-ordination and the responsibility for specific cases may be blurred creating a lack of ownership.

Experience shows that it is not possible to create unified conditions in some of these models (especially the first and third of those mentioned).

Cost effectiveness is also sub-optimal in such systems. It is difficult to utilize the large scale advantages. Double administration is to some extent built-in.

Again, the Third Insurance Directive might create problems for such organisations, and might also interfere with the creation of "framework" laws by governments.

The means of achieving clear-cut separation between incentive and compensation sides of the EMMI-body are complicated and probably not cost-efficient. The two sides of the body could be administered separately, but with a considerable co-ordination task.

5.3 Possibilities of variety and flexibility

In the previous sections we have discussed how the organisation behind the incentive scheme could be structured. There is, however, flexibility in the requirements for the organisation and variety in the way these can be met. In other words, the incentive methods and the necessary organisation are relatively independent.

Furthermore, national conditions differ significantly in terms of industrial sectors, labour markets and existing systems for prevention and workers' compensation. Each country could therefore develop its own version of the incentive scheme as well as choosing a different organisational structure for the administration.

A number of variables in the organisational structure can be considered:

○   Relationship to governmental authorities; the ministry responsible (social security, labour, trade and industry).

○   Separation of incentive scheme and compensation administration into two bodies.

○   Inspections and other types of visits to be made by other bodies licensed by the EMMI-body.

○   Using data from other authorities (for example, basic data on enterprises such as name, address, number of employees etc).

○   Division of industry into regions and/or sectors.

○   Special sectors freed from the obligation to carry insurance; self-insurance for parts of the state apparatus (military or the like).

○   Using a partition of enterprises into size groups reflecting differences in health and safety regulation (and safety organisation).

National features such as the size of industry, the country's geography and the labour market will often dictate the structure of the EMMI-body. Moreover, it has been assumed that inspection visits are central to the activities of the body, which leads to an obligation to operate at a local level.

Another feature that creates tension in the organisation of the EMMI-body is the dilemma between local and central organisation. Local organisation offers the possibility of designing "answers" to the local industry's problems, problems that develop dynamically. On the other hand the overall aims and planning of the EMMI-body may be better served by a centralised structure.

The key criterion for decentralisation of the organisation is however **uniform conditions**:

○ Enterprises with the same risks must pay the same rate. If several insurance bodies were acting (regionally or by industry) their premiums would have to be standardised.

○ The evaluation methods would have to be unified. The criteria for bonuses, investment aid etc. should be the same regardless of what part of the decentralised body treats the case.

○ Special sectors having other systems present a danger of treating similar working environments differently. The position could be, for example, that a military canteen ought to operate on the same incentive criteria as a civilian one.

Experience shows that splitting the organisation too much introduces considerable potential for systems to compete with each other with negative impact. The organisation requires regular procedures for co-ordination, joint training and other means to maintain the unification.

In general terms, our evaluation of the need for change in the EU-countries is that most countries need to go in the direction of more unified systems with less decentralisation.

5.4 Transnational relations

The EU creation of one free internal market, and the centralization of businesses operating transnationally and on the world-market, are developments that underline the need for enforced co-operation across borders. It is necessary to create a common policy directed towards multinational enterprises.

This is necessary in order to control these enterprises. They could be offered incentives and other schemes especially designed for them, but it is also necessary to avoid "social dumping" and the exploitation of national differences. At the same time international co-ordination and special incentives towards multinational firms should not lead to discrimination between national and international companies.

This does not necessarily involve harmonisation of the incentive scheme throughout the EU-countries. The common policy could be realized by establishing a forum for co-ordination between insurance bodies involved in specific transnational cases. This forum could be situated in an EU-body.

An option is to implement only parts of the incentive scheme at the EU-level. This could be the case for marketing labelling and for the financing of investment aid at community level.

The criteria for the marketing label could be unified through standardization work and the necessary further development of the label criteria could be divided among the different national insurance bodies.

The investment aid could be administered jointly by an EU-body and the local / regional insurance bodies in order to maintain the close contact with industry needed to implement the investment aid scheme. At the same time this arrangement would facilitate the collection of experience at both national and EU-level.

5.5 Conclusion

In this section we have described the requirements for the organisation. It has been emphasized that the incentive scheme and the necessary organisation are relatively independent. We have therefore described various options but have also emphasized our assessment that most EU-countries need to aim at a more unified model.

The wholly state-controlled model and the controlled independent institutions are the ones described as the most appropriate to the tasks at hand. But the choice of model is a national question and should be taken with due respect to existing systems.

Finally, co-ordination with the EU-level was discussed and some possible tasks for an EU-system were pointed out:

○ Helping the local insurance bodies to shape a common policy towards transnational businesses.

○ Funding the investment aid system and helping to monitor its experiences.

○ Co-ordinating the marketing label and promotion of common standards.

Implementation

6

6.1 Implementation topics

Introduction of the economic incentive model for improvement of the working environment in Europe requires the following:

○ The establishment of an EMMI organisation taking care of the organisational and administrative tasks to be performed in connection with the implementation of the model.

○ The establishment of a contract system vis-à-vis the enterprises to ensure that all enterprises participate, that the information is submitted and that the incentives gain influence.

○ The establishment of a social contract with the enterprises, the social partners and other bodies.

○ The establishment of a monitoring system, both quantitative and qualitative, to acquire up-to-date information from the enterprises and ensure regular updating of knowledge.

○ The development of an evaluation system for assessment of the actual risks in enterprises and for evaluation of the impact of working environment improvements on the risk level.

○ The recruitment, training and professional development of the staff who are to undertake the monitoring function and the risk assessments.

6.1.1 Establishing the insurance organisation

Section 5 contains a description and examples of the demands on the organisation capable of implementing the economic incentive model.

It is essential that the organisation behind EMMI becomes a public or semipublic body with a monopoly in the field, as stated already in Section 1.3.

It is also important the there is a clear connection and clear-cut distinction in responsibility between

1. the authority taking care of compensation for injuries arising due to a poor working environment

2. the safety and health prevention authority

3. the social security system and the health system as such.

The EMMI organisation can and must be capable of operating as a kind of bank or cash reserve. The enterprises pay to this "bank", and what they pay for is the risk to which employees are exposed at their enterprise. "The bank's" basis for collection is the methods described in the incentive model.

The money is then spent on payment of the costs incurred due to a poor working environment, including *inter alia*:

○ compensation for injuries that have arisen

○ treatment and rehabilitation of victims

○ inspection of the working environment

○ a prevention and advisory service

○ information and training in this field

○ research and development of new knowledge

○ investment aid

○ administrative expenses.

The size of the EMMI organisation may vary depending on the prevention and compensation systems that already exist.

EMMI may have a co-ordinating and managing function involving other organisations who will perform the actual tasks such as risk assessment, documentation, development of methods, etc.

On the other hand, EMMI could also be capable of handling all the tasks itself.

The latter would probably be the simplest approach from an efficiency point of view. However, when it is not a matter of starting from scratch but rather of building a system on top of an already very complex system, interim solutions may be more expedient.

6.1.2 Establishing a contract system

Section 3 described various incentive methods requiring a contract with individual enterpises.

It is necessary to develop and determine the form of contract to be applied by the EMMI-body and the enterprises, both in connection with premium payments and bonus awards and in connection with investment grants and labelling.

The contract must include information that makes it possible for

○ the enterprise to evaluate its own opportunities of obtaining a bonus, investment aid, labelling, etc.

○ the EMMI-body to evaluate the gross premium and the basis for offering an award of a bonus.

In addition to this, there are contractual rights and obligations, etc.

The contract must also state the way in which it is to be fulfilled. This report has discussed various methods. The most rational one will be to have as much information as possible submitted in writing. This will even be possible via an on-line system in the near future.

A system capable of providing inspections, evaluations, guidance and information directly to the individual enterprise concerning the final payments agreement will be necessary if an impact on prevention is really desired.

6.1.3 Establishing a social contract

Co-operation between the EMMI-body, the enterprises and other bodies needs to be based on mutual commitment, trust and understanding (the *social contract*). The social contract could be established by dissemination of information to enterprises and others about the new possibilities of the EMMI-incentives, but broader publicity should also be given about the obligations related to the contract and implications of co-operation. The dissemination of information could utilize TV, newspaper announcements, campaigning, local meetings etc.

6.1.4. Establishing a monitoring system

Section 4 describes a number of different needs and tools for monitoring of the working environment and risk factors.

Monitoring can take place through quantitative data as well as more qualitative knowledge.

Quantifiable data must be secured through register systems, spot checks and research results whereas qualitative knowledge must be obtained from other kinds of research (qualitative studies) and the experience of professionals. Professionals may be working environment professionals, researchers, method and process developers, public authorities, etc.

The establishment of registers permits statistical processing of information on:

○ *the consequences*, i.e. accidents, diseases, attrition and nuisances from work under high-risk conditions.

Examples of such registers are:
– registers of occupational accidents
– registers of diseases

- disablement registers
- treatment registers
- compensation registers

○ *exposure sources*, i.e. the occurrence of exposure factors in different enterprises, sectors, or working processes.

Examples are:
- working environment measurement databases
- product registrations
- workplace examination registers

○ *the enterprise and workforce*, its distribution by sector, trade, process, etc.

Examples are:
- enterprise registers
- workforce registers.

Important elements in establishing a complex of registers of the above nature are for them to cover the same population, to use the same identification for the same type of units and for the same classification methods to be used for the same information.

This can be ensured by using the same criteria across register systems and by developments, changes and levels being objectively measurable and calculable.

The establishment of spot checks and research studies will be necessary in order to acquire new knowledge and to measure in-depth the impact of changed production conditions, changed risk conditions, changed conduct, etc. Registers may give an indication of changes having taken place whereas mapping of what has happened and in what connection must be based on more scientific methods.

Finally, attention should be given to "softer" knowledge, qualitative information which professionals have within the various relevant fields. Regular follow-up of experiences, positive as well as negative, from

○ working environment professionals

○ process and product developers

- researchers
- public authorities

represents an important source for the continuous advance of knowledge about the working environment, its development and its consequences.

6.1.5 Establishing an assessment system

Section 4 described the need for a risk assessment system in connection with bonus calculations.

The assessment system must be based on established knowledge of the correlation between risk factors and the consequences experienced. However, it must always be possible to expand the assessment system by new knowledge obtained through either research or experience.

Several different types of assessment methods have been developed, the purpose of which is to describe risks at the workplace or when using machines. Examples are:

- Guidance on Risk Assessment at Work – EG/GD V/E/2

- Safety of machinery - Principles for Risk Assessment, European standard norm.

What is crucial concerning the evaluation method to be used for fixing bonus awards is that:

- There is a clear correlation between assessments and the quantitative fixing of bonus.

- There is objectivity in the assessments ensuring that the result is the same irrespective of the persons making them.

The biggest task is undoubtedly to carry out studies making it possible to quantify risk assessments.

An evaluation system will also have to be subject to ongoing development and follow-up on the evaluations carried through. In this way, it can be ensured that new knowledge on causal relationships forms part of the evaluations and it is possible to check whether existing knowledge still applies.

6.1.6. Recruitment and training

Section 6 described the qualifications to be expected of the persons who will perform the tasks of the EMMI-body.

Based on the existing employment and training systems, it seems obvious to recruit staff from the following fields:

○ the working environment prevention system

○ the traditional industrial injury insurance system.

Staff from the working environment system with knowledge of safety and health conditions will possess a large number of the qualifications needed for risk assessment, risk counselling, information on prevention, etc.

Staff from the industrial injury insurance system will be qualified in financial calculations seen from an insurance point of view and the associated statistical calculations. Moreover, this is where experience concerning financial administration, recognition of injuries, etc. is available.

The qualifications of both fields are necessary and must be integrated. Besides, new knowledge must be established and new evaluation methods must be developed which then have to be implemented *inter alia* through training of the staff.

6.2 Continuous Improvement

Hazards and risks at work are continuously evolving, due to decisions on the adoption of new technologies, new materials, intentional and unintentional effects of changes in organisation, personnel and their training.

Hence establishing the EMMI-body and the incentive scheme is a necessary but not sufficient precondition for the success of the prevention scheme. The EMMI-body and the incentive scheme are targeting a dynamic reality, so the EMMI-body must therefore aim at continuous improvement of its activities. These improvements could however be realized in a way that does not obstruct the decision-making in industry. In other words there could be a balance between the necessary improvements and the stability of the incentives offered to enterprises.

6.2.1 Improvement of monitoring

Improvements to monitoring should target the qualitative as well as the quantitative data.

Improvements of the quantitative data could be obtained by enhanced co-ordination with other authorities (e.g. the general health sector) or by including national and international scientific research results.

The task of preventing future risk necessitates close contacts with industrial practitioners. Networking health and safety professionals and other practitioners around the EMMI could be considered a system of early warning. This system could help EMMI to propose new areas for incentives and to specify bonus efforts. It is clear that the "monitored" data will be less valid than scientific research. On the other hand regular contacts with groups of practitioners could facilitate quick response to new developments in industry. As mentioned above the balance between improvement and stability is important for the success of the incentive scheme.

6.2.2 Improvement of the incentive scheme

Improvements to the incentive scheme could be a continuous agenda for the EMMI-work. All parts of the scheme could be evaluated regularly. Proposals for smaller improvements here and now could be collected by organising quality circles inside the EMMI-body as well as in conjunction with industry and other target groups. These committees could propose longer term changes as well.

External evaluation could be one instrument for improvements. These evaluations could, for example, collect target-group opinions and evaluate specific enterprise-projects.

Co-operation could be expanded to other possible partners. Consider the example of small enterprises. They often rely heavily on their banks. This co-operation could be enhanced by prevention/economic topics, which could involve co-operation between EMMI and the banks.

6.2.3 Improvement of organisation

The organisation of EMMI could be continuously developed. This includes all aspects from enterprise-visit strategies to training of staff. Enhancing the co-operation with the health and safety authorities might be one central topic.

Furthermore the utilization of information technology could be based on the prediction of continuous change. The systems could support existing routines as well as newly established ones.

Glossary and
References

GLOSSARY

Attrition. Non-specific cause of chronic injury.

EMMI. "European Model for Motivation by Incentives".

EMMI-body. The insurance organisation responsible for operating the incentive system.

Enterprise. Any public or private, commercial or industrial organisation, regardless of size.

EU. European Union; abbreviation used to reflect the European Community with the legal basis being the Maastricht treaty.

Incidence rate. The number of injuries in proportion to the size of the workforce, "size" being measured by the number of employees or the number of work hours.

Injury. Used throughout the text to encompass illness or disease as well as physical injury from accidents. See Section 4.1.

SME's. Small and Medium-Sized Enterprises.

Solidarity. Joint and several liability; the concept of sharing the risk between all the organisations in a sector.

Third Insurance Directive. Directive 92/49/EEC which regulates competition in the insurance market and provides for free trade. See Section 5.2.

Work function. Tasks performed by an employee. For example Production Functions are the human tasks carried out in production such as operating an assembly line.

REFERENCES

1   Catalogue of Economic Incentive Systems for the Improvement of
     the Working Environment, European Foundation for the
     Improvement of Living and Working Conditions, Dublin, 1994.
     ISBN 92-826-2705-5.

2   Economic Incentives to Improve the Working Environment,
     European Foundation for the Improvement of Living and Working
     Conditions, Dublin, 1994. Available in nine languages:-
     Spanish   ISBN 92-826-7681-1
     Danish   ISBN 92-826-7682-X
     German   ISBN 92-826-7683-8
     Greek   ISBN 92-826-7684-6
     English   ISBN 92-826-7685-4
     French   ISBN 92-826-7686-2
     Italian   ISBN 92-826-7687-0
     Dutch   ISBN 92-826-7688-9
     Portuguese   ISBN 92-826-7689-7
     Swedish   Follows
     Finnish   Follows

3   Economic Incentives to Improve Health and Safety at Work,
     Proceedings of an International Colloquium between Eastern and
     Western Europe, 12-14 October 1994, Warsaw. Publ. European
     Foundation for the Improvement of Living and Working
     Conditions, Dublin,1995. ISBN 92-826-9615-4.

CONTACT PERSON

The Foundation's Research Manager responsible for this project is:

Henrik Litske
Research Manager
European Foundation
   for the Improvement of Living and Working Conditions
Loughlinstown House
Shankill
Co. Dublin
Ireland

European Foundation for th̶ ̶ ̶ ̶ ̶ ̶ ̶ ̶rking Conditions

**An Innovative Ecor̶ ̶ ̶ ̶ ̶ ̶ ̶centive Model
for Improvement of the Working Environmer̶ ̶ ̶ Europe**

Luxembourg: Office for Official Publications of the European Communities

1995 – 108pp. – 14.8 cm x 21 cm

ISBN 92-827-4912-6

Price (excluding VAT) in Luxembourg: ECU 8,50